THE ANATOMY OF INTUITION

NURTURING YOUR SOUL'S GIFT

HELEN DAVITA

CONTENTS

DEVELOPING SPIRIT

INTRODUCTION

For most of us, intuition appears to manifest from out of nowhere. It may be accompanied by unexpected ideas, inspired thoughts, emotions, and sometimes physical sensations. However, when intuition presents, many will either dismiss it, seek a complex explanation of it, or an acceptance.

Too often, Intuition is disregarded, or worse, undervalued. For many, it is a trusty friend and a natural opportunity to evaluate something, somewhere or somebody.

The study of intuition is usually the domain of psychologists, anthropologists, and neuroscientists. The intentional application of intuition is not limited to, but a fundamental aspect of psychic and spiritual work too.

The aim of this book is to explore the theory, application, development and how on a personal level, intuition is a guide.

Coming from a spiritual teaching background, the primary focus is not on experiments and research, but on how it manifests and why that could be. Naturally there is a 'nod' to different theories, but personal experience is critical, because for each of us, our intuition is a unique font of wisdom.

Ultimately, whether spiritual or not, intuition is something we can all relate to at some point in our lives. We can all form hypotheses about it, but intuition cannot yet be measured scientifically, with predictable results. We can only experience it individually, to know it exists. Sometimes we find a consensus. For example, you find what appears to be your perfect house, in the ideal location and within budget. It ticks all your boxes. On viewing it, something you can't put your finger on, feels uncomfortable or just wrong. Later, you discover others felt the same, or that it takes a long time to sell.

One theory is that your discomfort is being invisibly broadcast and others are sensing it, from an invisible pool of emotions we tap in to unconsciously. Or perhaps you left a 'vibe' which imprinted itself energetically upon the fabric of the property, which others sensed when they viewed after you.

We try our best to either ignore intuition, or explain an insight with logic, reason, knowledge, social conditioning, and the expectations of our peers. Yet that becomes unsatisfactory when we cannot establish its origins and how insistent it feels. A strong intuitive experience is screaming for recognition. We can't shake it and the mind, body and soul are in a chorus of internal experiences.

Many recognise that 'gut feeling' or 'spidey' sense about something. Most of us remember a time when we ignored that inner 'knowing' and regretted it. So, is it right that we embrace it as one of our fabulous superpowers and put it to greater use? I believe it is. It exists so it is worthy of respect and discourse. Although we must proceed with an open mind, as logic, reasoning and science are our friends too.

Some of us can relate to meeting the new partner of a friend or relative and intuitively sensing they were not right for them. It leaves us with a feeling of unease around them. Many relationships do not last, but that does not mean that our intuition was wrong about a person if the relationship ends. We might claim our intuition was initially correct and regard the former partner as the problem - they never felt right. Statistics would prove otherwise in some cases - but not all the time.

We confuse ourselves because to remain loyal to our friends and family, we accept their choices, their journey, whilst we chastise our intuition. We give ourselves and others the benefit of doubt because we are intrinsically good people. But we dismiss the accuracy of our intuition when it is screaming at us to beware or to keep an open mind.

In the modern world, we rush around so much that we rarely stop to consider the significance of what we experience from moment to moment. We need to slow down if we are to recognise what our intuition reveals to us. It must be a vital area of our lives, because simply put - it happens spontaneously. It is beyond our control, and we always remember its significance, when we discover it served us well. Perhaps we remember the times we didn't listen to our intuition and wished we had?

Some won't respect our innate wisdom and 'survival kit,' known also as intuition. The scientific studies are important yet uncover more questions than answers. My experience of intuition differs from some academic models. For example:

In 2016, Galang Lufityanto, Chris Donkin & Joel Pearson, from the School of Psychology, The University of New South Wales, published their research on intuition. Entitled: *Measuring Intuition: Non conscious Emotional Information Boosts Decision Accuracy and Confidence.*

Their research is interesting, and it concludes: "***These findings support the notion that non conscious emotions can bias concurrent nonemotional behaviour—a process of intuition.***"[1]

Their experiment involved participants viewing a split screen. On one screen were moving dots and participants had to evaluate the direction the dots were moving. On the other screen were randomly scrambled, 'feel-good' images, such as cute puppies and kittens. They displayed the 'feel - good' images too rapidly for the participants to recognise them, yet the brain would still register what was shown.

The accuracy of tracking the direction of the dots was greatest when the cute images were shown, suggesting that positive emotions evoked by the unrecognised images, led to greater accuracy.

This is a different understanding of intuition as I know it. It makes sense that when we are feeling good; we achieve more. A positive mindset is a powerful mindset. It seeks challenges to overcome and blocks negative thinking. Yet consciously influencing the subconscious mind, wouldn't usually tally with my perspective on intuition.

There is a vast difference in my experience between intuition (an unexpected emotion, insight, sense, or realisation) and deliberate subliminal influences. Where I do agree with the scientists, is that intuition works well when we are calm, content and our minds are free of everyday distraction.

Intuitive states arise spontaneously and are difficult to ignore. Could they simply be engineered? There is a danger in this approach of discrediting all intuition to a state of scientific manipulation. Logic, knowledge, reason, and intellect are important states of the mind which all commune. Yet flashes of intuitive insight go far beyond the accuracy of watching some dots on a screen. Some intuitive insights save lives or change the world.

The experience of a friend demonstrated this to me a few years ago. As a professional mountaineer, she knew the dangers and risks involved, yet on one occasion, descended the mountain via the most treacherous and an unofficial route. She ignored the radio pleas from her base camp and descended at her peril, but with a trust that her intuition was right. She knew she had to do it this way, yet it went against all her years of experience, knowledge of the mountain, the terrain, and the sudden changes of weather systems. As she reached base camp, she learned an avalanche had unexpectedly destroyed the safer official route. Had she taken that route, she would not have survived.

This is the type of intuition I relate to. I recognise an intuitive, invisible communicating force, communicating with the soul about what it needs.

The soul, the subconscious and the conscious mind are working together. Therefore, influences are aplenty and isolating intuition from them is a challenge.

Albert Einstein also stated: "The only real valuable thing is intuition." For all the great inventors, mathematicians, philosophers etc., their starting point was an unexpected insight - a gut instinct, a knowing without procrastination. It came from somewhere invisible and arrived unexpectedly.

On the eve of his 'cracking the code' which would define modern physics, Einstein, and his friend Besso, went for a nature walk to discuss his unsolved problems about his theory of relativity. Einstein, distanced from home life and in natural surroundings vented his frustrations with his theory to his Besso, for the entire walk. There was something missing and he couldn't solve it.

The next morning, he arose early and whilst still waking, before he had a chance to think about his work, the missing piece intuitively fell into place, in a flash of insight. The theory of relativity was born and finalised by an intuitive moment!

Some things that do match the scientific approach to intuition, is that whilst Einstein was venting his frustration, he was lost to everyday thoughts, he was focussed on one issue. Interestingly, although he wasn't taking much notice of his surroundings, the positive influence of nature may be similar to the effect of 'feel good' images shown in the experiment with moving dots.

Focus, nature, and distraction could be key elements to inducing inspiration. This would explain why going for a walk is often the solution to clearing the mind and finding solutions.

We all have intuitive abilities. Some people find it easier to access and trust these abilities more than others. Having a positive attitude, a relaxed mind, an observation of how we are feeling, and trust helps us to be receptive to intuitive experiences. Understanding it further will lead to a greater respect for it and the potential to trust it more. Intuition is like a muscle that gets stronger with exercise and awareness.

Some people appear naturally gifted for their intuitive abilities, while others simply need to work harder to learn how to call upon this natural ability. Information received intuitively is often more complex than that received directly through the five senses of touch, taste, scent, vision, and sound. The power of one intuitive insight, can change everything for us.

Once you strengthen your own intuitive abilities, you will use them for your personal benefit and, with permission, they may benefit those who are close to you, if combined with psychic work, you will become more aware of interactions that are taking place around you and attuned to the wider possibilities' life offers.

Not everyone accepts the existence or relevance of intuitive abilities. Sometimes their religious beliefs prohibit or discourage them from being involved in intuitive activities. Others with a strong scientific background won't all consider intuitive abilities as significant because they're often unverifiable using scientific methods. Yet their interest in research - as Einstein believed, probably began with an unexpected flash of insight.

The terms "intuitive" and "spiritual" are commonly used interchangeably when describing a similar general field of experiences. Intuition is a unique, spontaneous event - whereas spiritual development typically refers to the way of life one chooses on the path to personal realisation. They can be complementary but are not the same.

Many view the work and abilities of psychics in a negative way. Yet a psychic does use their intuition extensively to achieve results and the ability of the psychic has been sought for millennia, in most cultures.

It's important with intuition, to remain objective with thoughts and subjective with feelings. We need to use logic too and take a step back - as if we are a third party to it. Intellect and a reasoning mind are part of our survival. If we remain only in a 'thinking; headspace, it denies the wonders of intuition. But if we try to exist solely on intuition, we can easily get confused when the mind is distracted and makes poor choices. A combination of intuition, logic and reasoning is natural, which is why it is important to explore intuition, as it is too easily dismissed.

I am a great believer about questioning everything and all I can state is that at this point of my journey, intuition is the language of the authentic soul.

Ultimately, mistakes will happen when you think you're reading or listening to something important intuitively. In fact, you might just be thinking of what you expect, or want to read or hear. Yet if you notice beyond the five senses - (including the ego that likes to take over and pretend it has intuitive abilities) your intuitive awareness grows. Your intuitive intelligence is mostly reliable, and you have an amazing superpower!

---

1. 1 Lufityanto G, Donkin C, Pearson J. Measuring Intuition: Nonconscious Emotional Information Boosts Decision Accuracy and Confidence. Psychol Sci. 2016 May;27(5):622-34. doi: 10.1177/0956797616629403. Epub 2016 Apr 6. PMID: 27052557.

PREFACE

His Royal Highness, The Prince of Wales (now King Charles III of the United Kingdom), addressed the delegates of the COP26 global climate conference, on the 2nd of November 2021 in Glasgow, Scotland. He spoke with passion about the need to protect the forests of the world.

As he spoke, he referenced the indigenous peoples of our world and how they understood intuitively and with a sixth sense, how to respect the cycles of life, nature, and the planet earth.

Whether you believe in global warming or not, we should respect, learn more about indigenous wisdom, and its ways of respecting all life. There is a chance the world might not be facing the catastrophe of climate change, had we done so. There is a likelihood, we would be making better decisions.

Industrialised societies ran amok with taking the lands from the indigenous tribes, plundering earth's resources, and selling them for profit, adding financial value to resources that are a vital for the planet's health.

We are all paying the price now, for we have lost or overlooked the wisdom and knowledge that stems from millennia of living aligned with our natural intuition. We are losing the holistic survival of the planet because we live by the norms of what has been called - civilised society. Now we must reawaken the forgotten or dismissed ways, to save ourselves and the planet. Intuition is so important that it is also about global survival.[1]

Many are seeking to understand responsible global needs and develop their innate skills to live more intuitively. More are giving up their modern lifestyles and seeking to live as close to nature, 'off grid.' Their soul intuition has guided them to seek a way of life, which brings them in to a closer alignment with nature.

Intuition is the common denominator of innate knowledge and inner communication. Many believe this could save us all from a material, industrial, and militarised world.

As Prince Charles's speech concluded, it reminded me how important it is to celebrate and nurture our intuition. How vital it is to accept we do have a sixth sense. How proud we should all be to know, trust and 'own' our intuition and use it for the greater good.

It is partly for these reasons I felt compelled to write this book. Science is enlightening, exciting, exacting, and measurable. However, it cannot replace the wisdom we are born into this world with, and has taught respect and survival to our ancestors. In this respect, we may be here today because of their intuitive lives.

Life is a giant hypothesis, but some things make sense when we learn to listen authentically. That listening is through intuition, and we all possess the ability to plug in to it.

Authentic intuition won't destroy our communities or the planet. We don't have to change our lifestyle to trust it more. It diversifies from the statistics, adds interest, enlightens, challenges us, and offers the human touch of the soul. It's time to bring it out of the shadows and be proud of our spiritual heritage. It's right to understand it better.

As you journey through the book, you will encounter the views of psychologists, psychics, intuitive practitioners, new and old. As we delve into the subject, we explore theories and common beliefs, associated with intuition.

A few chapters may appear as heavily weighted with theory. It's important to address as many areas as possible that influence intuition. Intuition is of genuine scientific and spiritual interest to the community too!

However, everything cannot be understood or explained, when it involves intuition. There is more to discover in the future. Therefore, there are many chapters dedicated to easily accessible intuition and its foundation, with plenty of fun and enlightening exercises to work with.

My perspective on the anatomy of intuition is through my personal experiences, shared wisdom, perceived wisdom, beliefs, academic study, and a career teaching intuitive and spiritual disciplines. Therefore I will also share a few personal insights.

As a teaching medium, I began my professional journey of spiritual development with evidential mediumship. I found it easier to make a connection to those in the spirit world, those who had lived before. I thought I didn't have the time or the need to work at an intuitive level, and that it was an unrefined form of spirit communication. I was wrong. I needed to understand how the energy of intuition manifests and soon realised that whilst communicating with the afterlife was amazing, people needed intuitive insights into their lives right now. I needed those insights too.

Furthermore, understanding and trusting your intuition shows you how to communicate authentically, and how to recognise in yourself that intuition and evidential mediumship, offer transferable skills.

Although I had known intuition all my life, I bypassed its development, until I came to a point in my work, where I had to step back and embrace intuition, to progress. Once I explored and incorporated more intuition to my life, my evidential mediumship progressed to a higher level.

I believe to understand intuition, is to understand and accept your unique mind, body and soul and the nuances of how they communicate non verbally. The language of spirit communication is universal. It transcends written and verbal languages and is in all cultures and communities.

When you recognise this and shift the focus to the afterlife, you are already in touch with the process, nature, messages and information that the soul is capable of communicating to yourself. You expand your ability and grow in confidence. To work with your intuition, I believe is to truly know your soul and what it needs to tell you, no matter who, what or where you choose to make a connection.

I have read what many others have to say about intuition and observed many students learning to trust it. We learn, adapt, adopt, reject, but ultimately, we gain wisdom from recognising our inner communication of intuition.

Intuition is a powerful factor in becoming wiser, because when it serves us well, we feel comfortable about ourselves. We grow in confidence. We trust ourselves.

For thousands of years, the humans who lived by incorporating intuition, have a head start on those of us who rediscovered it in our lives much later. My hope in life, is that we can bring together the timeless ancient wisdom of our ancestors and its relevance for today and tomorrow.

We consider intuition as our sixth sense. We usually count our senses as being five:

1. Sight

2. Sound

3. Smell

4. Touch

5. Taste

Intuition is a deeply personal experience, which makes it a powerful sixth sense to contend with.

I invite you on this journey through the book, one step at a time and to free your mind of expectation. It's easy to progress intuitive potential and with a few exercises, you will understand more about yourself.

Intuition has no appointment times - it just arises when the conditions are right. We just have to learn to listen to it.

Whatever your interest in intuition is, I hope you enjoy exploring it throughout this book. I also hope you recognise your own intuitive experiences, beliefs and thoughts that empower your life and make you the unique soul you were always intended to be - living your best life and trusting your own powerful wisdom.

We are naturally intuitive, and it is time to bring it out of the shadows, understand it, trust it, use it, empower your confidence, individuality and thrive.

1. 1 BY **DANIELA AGUILAR** ON 1 JUNE 2018 | TRANSLATED BY **SARAH ENGEL**

    Mongabay Series: Global Forests, Indigenous Peoples and Conservation

"The intuitive mind is a sacred gift and the rational mind is a faithful servant. We have created a society that honours the servant and has forgotten the gift." Albert Einstein

PART 1: THE INTUITIVE JOURNEY

There's a voice inside of us
That we often ignore
But it's always there for us
Trying to guide us towards what's right
If we'd only listen to it,
We'd always know what to do

1

THE WHISPER OF THE SOUL

Intuition is the whisper of the soul

Jiddhu Kirshnamurti

There is a universal language that all sensing beings are personally aware of. It expresses itself to each one of us through the power of intuition. The word intuition originates from the Latin 'in tuir.' This translates as 'knowing from within.'

Acknowledged in all cultures, tribes, species, herds, and individuals, intuition is our superpower.

If you are aware of your intuition at work, you may know that it communicates to you with feelings of:

- right or wrong,

- just or unjust,

- natural or unnatural

- trust or deceit

- wise or unwise

- safe or dangerous

- calm or anxious

- fear or safety

- confidence or insecurity

It could save your life, help you trust your decisions, assist others, find clarity and inner peace.

Intuition is natural because every being is also consciousness, navigating an eternal universe. This consciousness is communicated through our senses and perceived intuitively. It's the inner world of us all and under certain conditions, warns, informs, and helps us to feel.

We may think of our individual identity, as being a unique soul. Yet no soul is truly alone in the universe and of the many forms of communication, intuition is universally relevant to us all. It has no language barrier.

We all understand when someone tells us that they have a 'hunch' about something and yet how do you describe a hunch? We can't, but we all know what it means.

Intuition is a silent language connecting the vast abundance of the universal life force, the individual subconscious mind, physical body, heart, and soul. It speaks to us in surprising intervals from the primordial consciousness to the conscious mind and the heart.

The speed of intuitive transmission is impossible to measure but is experienced as instantaneous. This could be why developing psychics who use their intuition, are often taught to trust their first impression, rather than procrastinating over interpretations.

The fact that many academics have researched intuition, suggests that there is consensus that it is a force to be reckoned with. Intuition captures the attention of curious minds.

Intuition can be thought of as insight that arises spontaneously without conscious reasoning. Daniel Kahneman, who won a Nobel prize in economics for his work on human judgment and decision-making, has proposed that we have two different thought systems: system[1] is fast and intuitive; system 2 is slower and relies on reasoning. The fast system, he holds, is more prone to error. It has its place: it may increase the chance of survival by enabling us to anticipate serious threats and recognise promising opportunities. But the slower thought system, by engaging critical thinking and analysis, is less susceptible to producing bad decisions.

If we attempt to understand it for ourselves, learn when to trust it and know how to create the right conditions to experience it - intuition will be a respectable universal method of mind, body, and soul communication.

1. **Thinking Fast and Slow.** Daniel Kahneman. Farrar, Straus, and Giroux, 2011

2

THE INTUITIVE SOUL THEORY

There are many theories relating to the nature of our existence, relevant to intuition. Indigenous people, anthropologists, religious leaders, archaeologists, and many great scholars know that humans have always believed in an existence beyond this world. From the earliest cave paintings to ancient passage tombs, the belief that we are more than flesh and blood is undeniable and a constant in societies ancient and modern.

Before verbal language was discovered, humans survived with.

- Instinct

- Learning the natural laws of nature, the elements, and the environment

- Shared Wisdom from their ancestors and disseminated to future generations.

- Trusting our senses and feelings.

- Intuition

Yet the beliefs that a power greater than this world existed, and that life is a stage of a journey, is as constant today as it must have been thousands of years ago.

With many ways to explain this, we consider some common themes that have arisen throughout societies, cultures, religions both ancient and modern.

These themes include.

- A divine creative power

- A continuation of life after death

- An evolving, eternal, intelligent spirit consciousness

- An individual and a collective soul language

In some spiritual philosophies, we may consider the individual soul as an invisible, energetic aspect of our eternal spirit consciousness.

Our own eternal spirit is potentially an infinite expression of a divine power - or gods. We express our own eternal spirit in part, via the soul, during our earthly journey. The relationship between the spirit and soul is dynamic.

The uniqueness of the spirit and soul is significant. We may find identical characteristics in twins, for example. Yet they each have a unique soul mission in life. We may also find another soul who is totally 'in tune' with us and we call them our 'twin soul.' Yet - each of us is on a truly unique journey.

For those who experience what is often called a 'twin soul' in their lives, the theory is that there is such a thing as a collective consciousness. In other words, a likeminded, grouping of spirits and souls.

Every individual soul has potential for growth depending on what it gives and receives in life. It is food for their eternal spirit. No matter how similar a journey appears to another, there will always be points of divergence.

The individual soul simultaneously communicates with its invisible, eternal spirit. The spirit is our eternal contribution to our timeless, limitless universe.

The spirit is evolving and refining itself to be closer to the divine power. It intends to merge, which results in a state of true enlightenment and unconditional love. In the Buddhist tradition this is known as Nirvana.

On earth, the soul needs experiences, philosophies, and truths. These experiences feedback to its spirit. The element of the spirit, known as the incarnated soul, journeys to earth to complete a part of the spirit's evolution. The soul must contribute to the universal and eternal growth of its host spirit.

Every eternal spirit is constantly communicating with the divine, creative power (or universal life force). The life force, the spirit and soul complete the cycle of universal communication, whilst we are in the physical world.

The goal is that all become one, eventually. What would happen if that was achieved is beyond our imagination and knowledge. This is the great mystery of our life experience.

Imagine the human soul as a giant invisible satellite system, beaming packets of information back and forth - sending and receiving. Depending on what you do, what you send and receive, could influence your emotions, experiences, wisdom, spiritual progress and more. We relate it to the universal law of cause and effect.

We can only speculate how this all works. Everything is a hypothesis in life, yet from my experience and philosophy, this complex feedback system makes sense in an otherwise hypothetical existence. Spirit and soul depend on each other. The spirit being the wholeness and the soul its earthly ambassador.

One theory is that the universe developed from energy changes and, like many outstanding scientists have stated, energy is indestructible - it can only change form.

We also have different energies, such as physical, emotional, mental & spiritual. We also know of energies such as thermal, kinetic, chemical, nuclear, light, sound and electro - magnetic waves.

Ancient knowledge of energy, which is still accepted, applied, and studied today, includes the body energy determined by the actions of the chakra system. Here we have a system of energy stations within the body, communicating through invisible channels and affecting and reflecting our state of wellbeing.

Thoughts and actions are energy too, and indestructible. Every thought has an effect and alters the surrounding energetic environment. These alterations then continue to make further changes, and nothing stays the same. And so, the universe is constantly in a state of energetic changes and challenges.

As humans, access to the intuitive whisper of the soul is via the power of the mind, the stimulating energy of our environment, the body, the heart and all the senses, constantly inputting and outputting messages via the subconscious.

To know that power is to learn, listen, and respond to the energetic language of intuition and to how it manifests in each of us.

Sometimes we sense it almost physically, such as a 'gut' feeling, a lump in throat or a heaviness of the heart. Other times it is simply a knowing, via a mental image, a symbol, sound, colour, or scent.

We should all respect our intuition, no matter what we do with our lives. We cannot afford to ignore it. If we do - we lose sight of the gift of our eternal nature, the journey through life, the changing energetic impressions, our progress, and the space we hold in our limitless universe. Intuition is our guide and friend as we navigate the lessons of life and our quest for understanding.

Meaningful engagement with the intuitive soul results in us living authentically. For the soul doesn't lie, deceive, or cause harm. It has no time nor respect for egotistical motives. The soul is your unique birthright, and it expresses the truths you need to know. It is your inbuilt superpower!

We store all our thoughts, memories, and emotions in the subconscious mind, and here they merge with the soul. This aligns with the psychologists' view that intuition arises from the subconscious mental stimulus. If it arises from here, we are also at the soul point. Some may argue the subconscious mind and the soul, are one and the same. That may or may not be the case, but from a spiritual perspective, soul is our personal intuitive source.

When the soul recognises something that is aligned with its true spirit nature, we feel good, harmonious, empowered, positive, happy, abundant. The opposite may be true and when the soul is unaligned with something, we can feel negative emotions, fear, unbalanced, sad and lacking in personal power.

To thrive, we need a positive balance between our environment and the energetic health of the mind, body, and soul. We apply logical thinking, habitual routines, our beliefs, and the soul's authentic needs. When we find this balance, we are in harmony with our physical, emotional, mental, and spiritual needs. We make positive decisions; we are living towards our fullest potential and the reason we are here in the moment of 'now.' We are also sharing this with our spirit.

By deepening our intuitive awareness, we find it easier to maintain the balance with body, mind, and soul.

We can honour our true purpose and recognise what feels right.

Working intuitively, we know when a decision is for the greater good or not. As an intuitive serving others, your guidance is invaluable and encourages others to listen to their own soul's whisper.

3

EVERYDAY INTUITION

Your intuition is your guiding light in a busy, material world. From corporate business decisions, to knowing what your body needs - from choosing a new home, to finding an alternative route on a journey, intuition is a powerful guide.

Your intuition is revealed in moments when your conscious mind is not controlling your thoughts, expectations, and decisions. Sometimes it is a split second sense of something you can't put your finger on, when you least expect it. At other times, it could be an overwhelming sense that you can't 'shake,' until you decide whether to act upon it.

Intuition is most keenly felt when you are passively listening to your higher self, to nature and beyond. In other words, it often arises unexpectedly, when you are in harmony with yourself and with life. It arises in the silence between thoughts.

At other times, you may consciously take some moments when faced with a dilemma or difficult situation, to sense it. Sometimes we need to close our busy minds to the mental noise and allow our senses to reassure us. Intuition is natural to us all. We all experience it, but do we recognise it?

Consider these events:

- Have you ever had a 'gut feeling' about a situation, a person, or a future event, but couldn't understand why? Then later your inner sense proved you were right?

- Have you received a call, or a social media message from a friend, at the same moment you thought of them?

- Did you experience a feeling of heaviness or lightness when entering a room? Or a sense that something sad may have happened there?

- Have you 'gone along' with something you weren't comfortable with, despite it logically being a good idea and then it turned out to be negative experience?

- Have you ever had a strong feeling that someone you care about is in trouble and it turned out to be true?

- Perhaps you experienced a friend who 'appeared' happy with their life - but you just 'knew' it wasn't true. Later you discovered all was not well.

- Have you ever changed travel plans at the last moment, to discover your original plan ran in to problems?

- Do you get signs such as certain dreams or see certain symbols you associate something or someone with?

- Have you ever been instructed by your boss to do something that you know will turn out to be a bad decision?

If you answered yes to any of the above, your intuition was telling you something.

These are all signs your intuition is strong, and they may be a very powerful guide, when making decisions in life. If you aren't sure about something, the 'trust your gut' experience - is trying to help you find the clearest path towards happiness and success!

If you keep an open mind, remind yourself there is never a need for fear or repression about using your intuition. You should always consider everything that crosses your mind, even if it does seem a bit out of place at first glance. For even the thoughts we dismiss have helped us reach a decision, conclusion, or hypothesis worthy of consideration. Learning to truly listen to your thoughts and senses is an art. Knowing your personal truth is an intuitive process.

A true experience from many years ago:

I once lived in a top floor flat in the centre of York in the UK. One evening I was enjoying a coffee and looking out of the window at the street below. I saw a man walking past and I just couldn't take my eyes off him. I didn't know him, he looked normal, but I knew there was something not right about him. I felt compelled to watch him until he was out of sight. To this day I can remember everything about him from his clothes to his physique.

A couple of weeks later, I was watching 'Crimewatch', and the case of a man wanted for serious crimes against women was broadcast, along with the information that it was believed he had been in York recently. It was him of course, but it was intuition that told me he wasn't just another passer by - something was amiss. I had a compelling 'gut' reason to watch him intently. Yet at the time, I knew nothing about the crimes he had committed.

For most of our day we respond, make decisions and form opinions, based on a sense of logic, our experiences and reasoning.

We have seen many changes during the Covid -19 pandemic. By habit, education, and experience, many have turned away from their professions to lead a life aligned with what they intuitively know is their soul purpose. Being unable to take part in the work, in the way you once did and then having it suddenly stopped, has left time for reflection. Many have awoken to their soul's purpose during this time. They have listened intuitively because they have made choices that sustain happiness. For happiness is the superfood of the soul and it hears intuition like a beautiful piece of music.

Our sixth sense of intuition may or may not arise from the logical brain, but from the relationship between the subconscious mind, the body, soul, and spirit. Even the energy of places and situations will trigger intuitive responses. Yet while some may argue that intuition is existential to the human brain, it is always processed by the human brain and the body, so that we can recognise it.

It's true that the logic and reasoning processes of the mind and brain are important to our survival and functioning through life. It's simply that we are blessed with another sense, and it is our incredible intuition.

Do you also recall experiencing such a powerful intuition about a stranger and subsequently discovering there was great significance around them?

4

OBSERVING SKILLS FOR INTUITION

Becoming more observational in your life will encourage and strengthen your intuition. Observation is a form of mindfulness. You explore everything without attaching memories, preconceived ideas, former knowledge, or a consensus to your experiences. You accept it for what it is in the moment and how it affects you, without judgement.

As your observational skills grow, you notice that when your intuition is trying to tell you something, you automatically recall, when you had that felling before, and how it affected you. In time you won't even think about it - it becomes natural and when faced with a dilemma, you will know which solution feels right for you.

The first exercise is to observe yourself. You will need to be objective and imagine watching yourself as if it is someone else. The easier it is to detach from any analysis and simply observe, the greater the capacity to understand something for what it is.

When we assume our identity and routines are mundane or automatic, we stop observing objectively. We stop noticing things that are truly significant. It's as if we are on autopilot and have tunnel vision. Being consciously objective, our field of observation opens, and we see so much more. This exercise increases your field of awareness and prevents you from adding your expectations or assumptions.

Write down or record your answers and experiences. When you have finished, find a date three months from now. Then repeat this exercise and evaluate how or if your intuitive awareness has changed. In fact, come back to this exercise often. It is amazing what else you will 'see.'

The Observer in You

Please read through the exercise first.

In the evening, find a comfortable chair and have a pen and notebook nearby for when you have finished the exercise.

Take a few deep relaxing breaths.

You will imagine you are watching yourself go through your day. As you do this, also imagine yourself describing it to someone else.

Observe in your mind when you woke up this morning:

- How did you feel?

- What were your first thoughts?

- What made you wake up (a sound, the sunlight, someone, or something else)?

- What did you do after you woke up (apart from any personal care)?

- What did you eat and drink and how did you prepare this?

- What choices or decisions did you make?

Continue to review the rest of the day as an observer of it. Note anything significant, or unexpected that happened and how you felt about it. Try not to skip through the day and assume it was ordinary. See it for exactly how it was.

- Did you notice any moments when you suddenly changed your planned activity or a behaviour?

- Did you notice if you have any habits, you were unaware of?

- Were there any moments when you felt a strong emotion?

- Did you see anything that made you feel good?

- What did you eat? What did it taste like?

If you could go back in time and do a rerun of the day, is there anything you would have done differently today?

Review your day and write or record your experiences.

5

ARE YOU INTUITIVE OR PSYCHIC?

There is debate as to whether someone should call themselves an intuitive or a psychic. If we consider that the word 'psychic' is derived from ancient Greek *'psykhikos'* we discover that it relates to 'breath, spirit, soul, mind.' This would appear to be the ideal terminology for those engaged in either a psychic or intuitive experience. So why don't we just use the term psychic and ignore the debate?

Before we dismiss the term intuitive, a dictionary search explains that intuition, denotes, insight, spiritual perceptions.

'the ability to understand something instinctively, without the need for conscious reasoning.'

"we shall allow our intuition to guide us"

It would appear from this, that either term could be perceived as equally relevant, and for some it becomes a matter of preference. Whilst some may believe their preference is purist, there may be a tradition or school of thought behind it.

The Spiritualist tradition tends towards the term 'psychic' and refers to it as a faculty. In general, the 'new age' movement appears to prefer the term intuitive. On definition alone it, there are some common themes. Is it merely a fad to adopt a new name for it? Are we reinventing the same wheel? Is it mentally palatable?

Some feel that word 'psychic' has many negative connotations. It has been associated with frauds and is the term the mainstream press, tend to use when publishing a negative or derisory story about someone who works with their psychic ability.

Psychic is a term that has much ridicule attached to it. It is commonplace to hear people say, "I'm not psychic!" When they didn't know something. For many, the word psychic conjures up images of fortune telling gypsies, at the fair. It is sadly a term many in society have given a bad rap.

We should accept that for many people who are averse to psychics, intuition is acceptable - but is it accurate? Some are scared or disbelieving of the psychic world. If you are one who feels this way, with no interest in psychic phenomena, intuition is comfortable as it is available and natural to all. This is despite any beliefs or prejudices to the work of psychics.

'Intuitive' as a term, may also cause some confusion and detract from the soul connection that many associate it with. We hear of software and machinery that is also described as intuitive. The new technologies of artificial intelligence (A.I) are often marketed for their intuitive ability. They follow a complex set of algorithms to achieve what appears to be unique results. As clever as they are, they have no soul consciousness.

To clarify, intuition is something we are all born with, but psychic skills are broader and developed to help others too. The skilled psychic will have developed their intuition significantly and rely upon it to do enhanced psychic work.

To be a psychic, you will also be intuitive. But to be an intuitive, you don't have to develop your deeper psychic skills, (often required to intuitively read another person's information). In this case, we may determine that intuition is the communicator, and the psychic is the interpreter.

Some claim that you are either born with psychic ability - or not. Not everyone is psychic if this is the case? I believe we are all born with psychic ability, to a greater or lesser extent. But whether you feel compelled to develop it and incorporate your intuition this way, is personal choice. A skilled psychic must be also be highly intuitive.

One major difference is that everyone experiences intuition at some point in their lives. We have all known that 'gut feeling.'

The psychic sees intuition as a tool of internal soul communication. If it is how many psychologists believe - a process of subconscious stimulation, the psychic is using this internal experience and has developed the ability to 'listen' to it when sensing people, situations, objects, animals, place and much more.

Whatever your feelings about the psychic/intuitive name tag, we ALL experience intuition in our lives and it starts from an early age regardless.

6

THE INTUITIVE CHILD

The phrase 'out of the mouths of babes' is one we are probably familiar with. At some point we will have experienced profound insights from children. Our response is often to describe them as 'a young head on old shoulders.' Those who believe in reincarnation may also associate such insight to a past life experience.

The past lives explanation is understood and believed by many. There exist incredible stories from children who appear to believe they have lived a life before, and if not, receive some knowledge from a source that cannot be defined. It could be that we have all had a past life, but there are a couple of common factors with Einstein's eureka moment on the theory of relativity.

Most pre - school children function in the present moment. It possibly explains why summers are remembered as longer and hotter. The child relates to a time of year when they experienced many moments of joy in nature, whilst the weather was warm. They are free of distracting everyday thoughts and focussed on each moment of play. These moments feel timeless.

When children go to school they are introduced to terms, holidays schedules, specific lessons at a set time and standard break times. They are encouraged to learn with logic, reasoning, intellect, and a standardised curriculum.

This is done carefully with the youngest pupils, who have more creative (and intuitive) experiences in the classroom, through art and storytelling. The young mind is gently introduced to actives which include, counting, reading, writing, and listening. As they get older, the curriculum eventually leads to testing their knowledge, competing with their peers, or a benchmark of results and a belief that achieving in the school system, determines their futures.

This is a huge adjustment for the highly intuitive child, who lives in the present moment. Yet we need to nurture all states of mind, whether logic, reasoning, knowledge, intellect, intuitive insight, and creativity.

Highly intuitive children have a deep empathy and social conscience. Their world is creative and their insights beyond anything they have seen, heard, or been taught.

Some other common traits of highly intuitive children include:

- Frequent daydreaming

- Invisible friends

- A fascination or fear of the dark

- Difficulty focussing on tasks they haven't chosen for themselves

- When focussed on an activity, find it stressful to be interrupted

- Creatively artistic

- Learns to play musical instruments by themselves

- Appear to know information that hasn't been taught to them

- Claim to see spirits and speaks to them

- Emotionally sensitive

- A need to protect and care for animals, plants, and nature

- May find it difficult to fit in with large groups

- Tries to heal everything from worms to humans and loves receiving healing therapies

- Often tend to be visual learners

From my own experience of parenthood, I witnessed my son on many occasions share his intuitive abilities and astound me with his wisdom. I am sure most of us can relate to the following experiences if we spend enough time in the presence of young minds.

At around the age of two, as I read him a story in bed, he asked me to stop reading and listen to him. He sat up and placed a hand on each side of my head. Then announced my newly emerged silvery grey streaks were called wisdom hairs, and he was proud I had them!

I asked myself how he knew that age affected my changing hair colour and why this ageing would be seen as a sign of wisdom? I certainly can't remember us ever having a conversation about greying hair colour or that age denoted greater wisdom. I'm sure at the age of two, nobody had explained to him what wisdom meant.

At the age of three I took him swimming one day. As we played in the pool, I briefly glanced an obese woman walking along the poolside, toward the pool steps. My son started pointing at her and shouting that I must look at her. I pretended I hadn't heard at first and turned him around, so she was out of his sight. He insisted I looked and was shouting at me to look. He held my face in his hands and physically turned my face towards her. I felt embarrassed.

We are so often judged on physical appearance and obesity carries its share of negative assumptions and confidence issues. I told him it was rude to point and stare at someone we don't know. His reply was "but she had the most beautiful face and I needed you to see her beauty!" Something within in told him that she was beautiful and that he needed to share this with me. That was all he saw - her beauty, whilst I was concerned about prejudice and embarrassment.

I learned a lot from a three year old that day. I should have trusted and been intuitive about his insistence as I had no reason to doubt that something was very important to him. I put peer prejudice about physical appearance before the wisdom of a toddler.

As a toddler, my son was a typical hyperactive boy, but one thing I could count upon to settle him, was by giving him Reiki - Japanese spiritual healing. He responded to the intentional energy flow of healing and the placing of hands on his head. Within seconds he would be calm for the rest of the day or fall asleep at night within minutes.

If we look to the children, we may see what many adults have lost. Children don't question their intuition and naturally gravitate to inspiring or healing energies.

As examples to the young, it's important to listen and learn from their intuitive insights. It's vital that when they enter mainstream education, we ensure their creative activities are plentiful and there is balance in their lives. When they move towards a standardised curriculum, we can balance their lives at home, with more opportunities to play creatively and trust the little voice inside ourselves, as a friend. We must let them grow with the knowledge that their intuition and how it expresses itself, is something to be proud of and complementary to all their new knowledge.

Nurturing The Intuitive Child

As individuals who have the honour of being in the presence of young children, such as parents or caretakers, it is crucial to acknowledge and nurture the innate gift of intuition. How can we ensure that this invaluable trait is not neglected and adequately communicated to our children? Here are some ideas:

1. Describe it as "inner knowledge" which refers to a deep understanding we all have. This intuitive sense acts as a friend, consistently offering guidance and solutions.

2. Empower them with the knowledge that listening is not limited to the ears alone. The power of listening

resides in the entire body. Pay attention to how the body feels, does it feel constricted? Are they experiencing anger or fear? Is their stomach churning? Remember, the body is always honest and will alert when something isn't right. Trust the body and let it guide towards the truth. Believe in the self, and they will retain the power of profound listening.

3. It's important to give kids the space to express their emotions and thoughts, and when they do, show them some love and recognition. By doing so, we help them avoid the pitfalls of second-guessing themselves and feeling lost when it comes to making choices. Let's empower our young ones to trust their own instincts and stay true to themselves!

4. Teach children to know the difference between imagination and intuition. Encourage imagination, yet empower the child to know that they can control it. They create the stories in their minds. With intuition, it is a natural unshakeable and uncontrollable feeling.

As you witness a child's realisation that their thoughts and insights hold value, no matter their size or age, guide them towards the brilliance of their own inner knowledge. Encourage them to trust their intuition and what feels most true to their heart. For within themselves, lies the wisdom and guidance they need to navigate this beautiful journey of life.

7

INTUITIVE CHOICES

Welcoming your natural intuition can empower you in everyday situations. It can be as simple as making a rapid decision, trusting it, and accepting that whatever the outcome, you owned that decision. You took personal responsibility.

Imagine you are driving to an important hospital appointment. The traffic has been heavy and according to your satnav, you will arrive at exactly the time of your appointment. You know you need to find a parking space and it will be a rushed experience. You can feel the stress rising in your body and you begin to feel anxious.

As you approach a 'T' junction, your satnav shows you will need to turn left. However, the artificial voice unexpectedly tells you there is an alternative route and that if you turn right, the journey is five minutes shorter.

The dilemma is that if you turn right to save five minutes, you are on unfamiliar roads. Turning left is a route you already know well.

Behind you, drivers are honking their horns at you adding to the stress. You must decide now. Which way will you turn?

What would you decide to do?

However, there was a third way forward and in deciding which direction, you can quickly clear your mind by taking a breath and asking yourself - which way feels right for you and trusting the feeling. Doing this would mean adding your intuition to the decision. It can be a big help as it's the one thing we can take personal responsibility with.

We can't control the traffic, but we can trust ourselves to try to do what felt like the right decision. That always feels better. It's empowering, it's natural and at least even when it doesn't always work in our favour - you took responsibility. You owned the decision. You couldn't blame the satnav, the traffic, or the impatience of the drivers behind you. You took them all into account subconsciously, yet you had a choice to act upon your intuition.

If it works out badly for you and you arrive late for your appointment, you can shrug your shoulders and face the consequences. If you trusted the satnav, and it took you on the wrong route you will be more stressed, possibly frustrated, and angry. If you swore at the impatient drivers, it didn't get you there any faster and it made you stressed.

The secret is to remember to add your intuition to decisions and situations. It's your personal empowerment in your decision making process and part of a complex set of instructions we are constantly receiving and responding to.

Intuition tends to arise when your soul reacts to thoughts, feelings, senses, and energies. The guidance and wisdom we receive intuitively, is beyond conscious anticipation.

Some years ago, when I was teaching at the Arthur Findlay College, one of my students from Australia, talked about eating intuitively. She was from Australia and explained that she had experienced a serious illness. The treatment had left her very overweight, and she decided to sit in meditation and ask for an answer to help her regain her previously healthy physique. She told me that the answer she received was to eat intuitively.

To start this process, she learned about energy healing, as she felt it would help her understand intuitive energy.

At lunchtime, I saw her at the buffet and witnessed her gently sweeping her hand across all the food choices. She then put a few items on her plate and noticed me watching her. I asked if that's all she does and she said yes. She explained that she trusted the intuitive energy to guide her to what her body needs and now she was a healthy weight again.

Fast forward four years and I was teaching at a seminar in Australia with Tony Stockwell and Lyn Probert. The same student was there too, and I asked if she remembered the previous conversation. She remembered and was using her intuition in other areas of her life now. She was healthier, happier, and full of a lovely self confidence that inspires others.

Exercises on choices:

Start your awareness with simple decisions, such as food or shopping choices. For example:

• You are looking at the menu of your favourite restaurant. Put all thoughts out of your mind of what you usually order and with each meal description, read about them, focussing carefully on each description and every ingredient. Put the menu out of sight, take a breath and ask yourself which meal description will provide what I need at this time? That's the one to choose this time.

• You are in the supermarket and buying a tin of beans. There are three choices which are all the same price - your usual brand, the store brand, and a new brand you haven't tried before. Pick up your usual tin and become aware of how you feel about it. Why do you normally buy this brand? Put it down, take a breath and then pick up the next tin. Do the same - does it feel different to your usual brand? How do you feel if not? Do the same with the third tin - the new brand. Now with them all back on the shelf take a breath and intuitively reach for the right tin!

You don't need to do this with everything you eat or buy, all the time. Adapt the concept of the exercise to other areas of your life. As your confidence in your intuition grows, it becomes natural. Of course, there are times when your budget and the wishes of others will influence your choices. But a simple experiment like this now and again may yield some interesting results. Moreover, you will strengthen your trust in yourself.

8

WHEN YOU KNOW - A PERSONAL EXPERIENCE

An event from my twenties that I remember vividly was when my intuition became very real and reliable to me. It has stayed with me ever since, and it's something that I always appreciate as a lesson to trust my inner knowledge.

I worked for a city council in the social services sector. I looked after a specific area of the city where my job was to oversee and advocate for welfare of vulnerable people in the community.

On an average day, I visited my clients, checked they were ok, made referrals to other caring organisations for help if needed, called for GP visits as needed and sometimes had a cup of tea with those isolated in their homes. Back at HQ, I made applications for grants and liaised with other professionals on behalf of the clients.

I had to respond to emergencies and deal with whatever I encountered. Often this was a case of neighbours reporting someone hadn't been seen for a while, or direct calls from people who had fallen and were injured. I had a walkie talkie and car to move quickly if necessary.

The clients had buttons on a cord around their neck, that would send an alarm signal to HQ when pressed.

The signal would then be received and responded to by HQ, who would alert me via my walkie talkie.

The most vulnerable clients, also received a call every morning to check on their welfare. If there was no response from a vulnerable client in the morning, the control room operators would try again later. If there still was no response, then an instruction with a key to enter the property would be granted.

On a particular weekend, I was called to check on an elderly man who was outside of my usual catchment area. I was not familiar with his general situation.

We stored keys for those without family living close to them. Although the client had family who were his key holders and first point of contact if there were any concerns.

Unfortunately, the family didn't answer the phone when we called them, after there had been no response from his morning check in and recheck. I received a radio message to attend the property, establish if he was there, and if I could determine that he was ok.

As I approached the front door, I saw a pint of milk on the doorstep. It was a Sunday, so I knew it wasn't delivered that day as the milkman only delivered Monday to Saturday. I radioed my concern in.

My next task was to see if anyone inside the property could respond to me. I knocked hard, shouted through the letterbox, listened intently, and felt sure he was inside, despite no response from him.

His dog was mournfully howling back at me from the other side of the door.

I couldn't see inside the home because of its net curtains, solid front and rear doors, and draught excluder on back of the letterbox. I radioed my concerns back to the control room.

Meanwhile, they kept calling the key holder in the hope someone would answer soon and put our minds at rest.

Where we suspected someone was in trouble and needed urgent attention, we would often call the police and ask for permission to break into the home via a window, if we were not the key holder.

We had to meet certain criteria for this request to be agreed. Sometimes the police attended, but many times when they were busy, and they left us to do this ourselves.

I felt so strongly that he was inside, and we needed to get that police consent.

There were a couple of things to check out to meet the criteria - witness sightings were priority. I called next door and asked if they had seen him lately. One person responded that his family often came for him and took him out for the day and was certain they had seen them do this. I asked if he always left the dog, to which they replied yes. Does the dog normally howl? I asked. The answer was a resounding yes.

It gave me my last chance to find a reason to get permission to break a window and enter the house when I found the pint of milk on the doorstep. The neighbours stated it was normal for him to forget to bring it in. Scuppered!

I had run out of criteria, but I knew he was inside, either in trouble or deceased.

The control room staff had no justification for keeping me there any longer, and they instructed me to go home.

The next morning, his daughter visited and found him dead in his chair. They had come home late on Sunday night from a day out with the grandchildren and in the morning, realised their telephone had several messages from the control room concerned about his welfare. They went straight to his home and found him.

I just knew he was inside his home all along and nothing shook me from this knowledge. I can't tell you how I knew - other than a very strong intuition. There was nothing to see, no odour or human sound that alerted me. The neighbour's witness reports countered every possibility that suggested he was still inside.

It was pure intuition that convinced me he was there. Logic and reasoning were unhelpful in this case.

According to the coroner, he had passed on the Friday evening, so had been dead for almost two days by the time I was on the scene.

I will never forget the strength of feeling that he was there all along. The power of intuition can be subtle, but sometimes it totally overwhelms. When you know - you just know. You may not be able to change a situation, but when that knowing seems unshakeable, you know you can absolutely trust your intuition.

9

THE CONSCIOUSNESS

As previously alluded to, your state of consciousness is fundamental to how receptive you are to your intuition.

Consciousness refers to the state of being aware of and able to think, feel and perceive. It is the ability to be aware of your surroundings and make decisions. It is what allows us to interact with the world around us.

Fundamentally, there are two primary functional levels of human awareness. These are generally recognised as the conscious, and unconscious states. Simply put, they are the two states in which we are either aware of our thoughts and environment, or not at all! Aware versus unaware - awake versus asleep.

However, a third intermediate level, influencing our mind is known as the subconscious. I alluded to the subconscious mind in the chapter: The Whisper of The Soul -

"We gather all our thoughts, memories, and emotions in the subconscious mind..."

The Psychoanalyst Sigmund Freud, referred to three levels of consciousness:

- Consciousness

- Subconsciousness

- Unconsciousness

The conscious level: The conscious level is the level of awareness that people are aware of at any given time. This is the level where people are aware of their surroundings and can make decisions.

The subconscious level: The subconscious level is the level where people store memories and automatic responses. This level is usually outside of a person's functional awareness, but can be accessed through techniques of hypnosis, meditation, and deep relaxation.

The unconscious level: The unconscious level is the deepest layer of consciousness and contains a person's instincts and drives. This level is usually not accessible to a person's conscious mind but can be revealed through dream interpretation or psychotherapy, according to Freud.

However, Freud's student Carl Gustav Jung (who became an eminent psychoanalyst himself), explored further and referred to another level on consciousness, which he called the superconscious level.

The superconscious level: The superconscious mind is a term used in psychology to describe a state of mind that is beyond the subconscious mind. It is considered by some to also be the spiritual source of intuition and creativity, and it is said to be capable of also harnessing the power of the subconscious mind. Some people believe that the superconscious state, can be used to connect with higher divine powers or spiritual realms.

10

INTUITIVE INTERFERENCES

When 'intuitive' or psychic impressions are perceived as beyond the threshold of normal awareness, they may not be as authentic as we first thought. Our senses are constantly receiving information, even when asleep. However, marketing companies have capitalised on something known as subliminal advertising and as humans we also have imagination, delusion, and an ego to challenge authentic intuition.

Subliminal activity generally works by subconsciously stimulating your senses. Sometimes is occurs naturally, such as walking into a coffee shop with freshly brewed coffee. As the fresh aroma arouses your sense of smell, it's hard to resist buying one! Freshly baked bread or cakes are another great example of the senses reacting and then convincing us to buy and eat. The old trick of brewing fresh coffee or baking bread sells houses!

In another example, diet programs often recommend that grocery shopping should be avoided on an empty stomach, so as not to buy too much — as the power of suggestion is tempting, particularly through the five senses.

Subliminal advertising was banned in the USA in1958. Companies such as Coca Cola, KFC, and Marlboro cigarettes, attempted to bypass the law and used imagery to psychologically persuade customers to buy their brands. For example:

A KFC burger advertisement featured a small layer of salad greens. In fact, if you looked carefully, you could see that within this green area was a minute image of a dollar bill.

With Coca cola, they advertised a bottle of coke surrounded by ice cubes. If you looked carefully behind one of the ice cubes, a pornographic image of a woman could be seen. It was difficult to spot but the eye would have 'picked it up' and the brain registered it.

Marlboro cigarettes thought they were being very clever within motorsport. The company had a long held advertising association with motorsport sponsorship. Advertising on formula 1 cars was banned in 2006, but to bypass this, they left a barcode logo. If you saw it pass your eyes at speed, it could appear to signify Marlboro cigarettes.

From the intuitive perspective, the distinction between subliminal information and genuine intuition appears thin. As intuitives we must develop the ability to know that the information has the 'right' energy and is not gained from anything that has been deliberately manipulated. With real intuitive experiences, this shouldn't happen.

Subliminal intent is generally used for advertising purposes, entertainment, or deception — such as with fake mind readers. However, an awareness of the power to influence the mind is important if we are to gain confidence with our own intuitive nature.

Some intuitives, confuse what first arises as a 'mental chatter,' to be intuitive knowledge. Basically, some will repeat what first comes to their mind. Yet the mind is rich with subconscious experiences, memories, perceptions, prejudices and is powerfully imaginative. There is no intent to deceive here — merely a lack of intuitive recognition, which can be corrected with experience.

Others, offer information that appears to be accepted as psychic, yet is simply general information most of us relate to. A fraud will use this method of generalisation to appear to have an inner knowledge. Most are not frauds, but an intuitive may be working this way by default, from falling into lazy habits. It needs remediation through further development.

The waters can become muddied very quickly when we solely work intuitively. Events, images, words, songs, feelings etc can all trigger thoughts and memories that reside subconsciously and influence our personal thoughts.

The key is knowing when the trigger is a personal association, assumption, wish fulfilment, or a genuine attempt of the soul, mind, and brain to draw your attention and offer an intuitive experience. Authentic intuitive impressions develop rapidly without thought and are often surprising to us.

Questioning everything is key, but staying grounded, rational, and balanced is vital for working with intuition. When we do this, we are less likely to mistake an intuitive impression, from a personal trigger or unrelated subconscious influence. We must know the power of the minds we possess.

11

GROUNDING

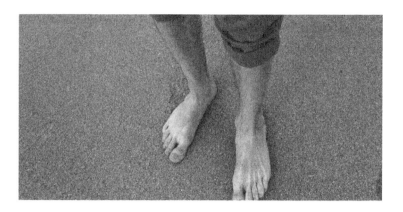

In much intuitive work, it is common to hear about the subject of grounding. Some teachers of intuition instil in their students that they must practice complex grounding exercises as part of their development.

It is as if they will fly off the ground in a wildly, uncontrolled manner and suffer greatly, if they don't!

Having spent many years working as a spiritual and intuitive development teacher, students were sometimes perplexed at the scant time given to grounding exercises on their courses. It was as if they were being led into unsafe territory, if a 'grounding' meditation or exercise didn't follow every session.

Yet unbeknownst to some, the group feedback, and regular breaks for coffee, was a natural grounding technique. Conversely, the topic of grounding, received ridicule from some teaching peers, and it is important to be clear on the subject.

Grounding is important, but especially when a person has been working in an altered state of awareness. For example, I taught many courses on trance mediumship. This involved exercises which were about experiencing an altered state of awareness. By the end of a teaching day, most of us felt like we could float home without a care in the world. Getting into a car and driving home in this state is obviously dangerous. It was vital to spend some time grounding' at the end of the day, so that everyone felt totally physically and mentally aware.

It makes sense that when there is an abundance of energy, it must find an exit when it reaches a critical level. Similarly, low energy needs to build its power to become effective. Intuitives are in the business of working with energy and energy awareness is vital.

In nature, we can look to electrical storms to demonstrate how natural grounding is. Lightning needs to ground itself and finds the easiest route it can to discharge its power.

The advice never to stand under a tree during an electrical storm, is paramount. The excessive electricity has a pathway through the tree, into the roots and then into the ground.

In the home, the electrical system also needs a route where any surges of power can be discharged into the ground. This form of grounding is also called earthing. Modern house systems are equipped with fuses, to prevent dangerous electrical energy surges potentially causing a fire or electrocution.

Grounding or earthing is natural and necessary and relevant to intuitives, and others involved with any form of spiritual work, with a need for a safe release of excess energy.

With grounding exercises and activities, you can do as many as you wish, spend as long as you need, but one activity lasting a few seconds, may be enough to help you feel grounded again. Keeping it simple will help. Also, make a note of how you feel before and after your grounding practice.

Much of the time we are unaware of naturally grounding ourselves. It is what we are meant to do. It comes naturally. Conversations about nature, stroking an animal, inhaling the sea air deeply, admiring a tree or flower - are all grounding us on an unconscious level. Because it is natural, there will be many times, after engaging in intuitive work, you have naturally grounded yourself.

However, if you feel out of sorts from working intuitively, a conscious activity may help. The following are based on the natural phenomena of a need to find a good conductor of energy. This is so any excess energy can find a safe path.

Grounding Exercises

Water:

- Drink fresh water and with each sip, be mindful of its refreshing quality

- Rinse your hands under a running tap for a few seconds

- Use a spray mist on your face if you need to awaken more

- Walk barefoot on wet grass (a walk barefoot in the grass early morning is a great way to start the day)

- Paddling in the sea or have a foot bath

Earth:

- Place you hand on the soil, scoop some up and notice its texture, moisture, weight, colour etc.

- Yes hug that tree, or if you feel a bit silly, lean against it and be mindful of its size, temperature, texture, how it moves etc
- Walk with barefoot on soil or sand
- Plant a seed
- Hold a small pebble or some quartz rock

Metal:

- Touch something which is metal such as jewellery, cutlery, an office cabinet - anything which is metal but not connected to an electrical supply. Excess static electrical buildup will disperse this way
- Metals such as gold, copper and iron are all great conductors and holding a piece of jewellery or a coin will also help discharge a build up of electro - magnetic energy

Air:

- Opening a window or a door will move, refresh and replace the atmospheric nature of a room - especially if it feels highly charged
- A few good breaths will help too
- Air is movement and moving the body, displaces the air and changes the biological activity, chaining the electro - magnetic field

As we can see, grounding can be so simple and there is no need to create complex rituals, when it comes to feeling more connected with the physical world.

In the next chapter, there is an extended balancing exercise. Some intuitives benefit from a longer activity which helps them feel both connected and in balance - especially when developing their intuition, or at times when working with becomes intense.

PART 2: STATES OF ENERGY & HUMAN INFLUENCE

12

THE FOUR ENERGY STATES: PHYSICAL, MENTAL, EMOTIONAL AND SPIRITUAL

physical	mental	emotional	spiritual
Environment	Attitudes	Feelings	Spirituality
Health	Beliefs	Fears	Divine connections
Family/friends	Knowledge	Hopes	Spirit
Home	Decision making	Dreams	Soul
Work			
Animals			
Nature			

Aspects relating to the physical, mental, emotional and spiritual states of energy

Understanding and working with intuition is complex, as there is much we still don't understand. With what we do understand so far, there is a method which can simplify it and break it in to manageable parts.

To do this we consider four defined intuitive energy states:

- physical

- mental

- emotional

- spiritual.

We need them all working together, yet they don't have to be explored all at the same moment. Nor do they need to be experienced in equal measure.

We can break them down as distinct areas to make sense of them. If we remember that each state signifies and defines a different type of energy, it becomes easier to focus on their qualities and what it means to us.

Trying to make sense of something on several levels, often leads to overwhelming impressions and important information is at risk of being generalised, overlooked, or easily forgotten. It's overwhelming for us to compute everything at once. Therefore, we could separate intuition into energy states (or distinct areas), which we can focus on one at a time. Later we can build the larger picture when we have greater experience and recognition of them.

It would be easier and descriptive, to consider the four intuitive states as:

- The physical intuition

- The mental intuition

- The emotional intuition

- The spiritual intuition

Once we understand what the four realms could represent, it is easier to work through what is happening intuitively, and systematically. The method that makes logical sense. At a basic level we can begin to ask ourselves:

- PHYSICAL: How is this feeling or situation affecting me in my body, my relationships, my home, may daily life etc?

- MENTAL: What do I think and what knowledge do I bring to it?

- EMOTIONAL: How is it making me feel?

- SPIRITUAL: Does it relate to my spiritual beliefs and knowledge?

You can also replace 'me' and 'my' for 'them' and 'theirs' if helping someone else with an intuitive reading.

The importance of this intuitive energy and its place in our lives, makes sense when subdivided and we can start to begin the good work. We can explore how helpful this could be.

1. Physical Intuition

The physical intuition can be subdivided into the instinctive survival aspect and subsequently, its environment. We must start with the instinctive primal state, as although it is not something an intuitive can work with subjectively, (it responds uniquely to the individual animal and without conscious control), it is important to the overall understanding of us as human sentient, animals.

1.a Physical - Instinctive - Primal States of Energy - Unconscious Control

In our most fundamental physical state, our brain contains a survival system known as the 'primitive' system. It's located deep in the skull and is mostly concerned with important physiological functions, such as breathing, heart rate, blood pressure - essentially anything vital to sustaining life.

If something puts your immediate survival in jeopardy, this part of your brain will trigger a powerful response until you're safe again. This functioning of this part of the brain makes a difference between life or death. It relates to our primal instinctive responses of either:

- Flight

- Fight

- Freeze

The primitive brain in your body is purely instinctive and functions almost like a giant antenna picking up all kinds of signals. When it senses danger, it immediately triggers what's called the sympathetic nervous system.

When this is activated, you receive a boosted response. This bypasses normal conscious thoughts and makes you react quickly, without having to think, relate to a specific store of knowledge, or apply reason.

For example, your heart rate and breathing will increase to prepare the muscles of body for fleeing the situation rapidly. This could occur in a scenario when there is an emergency, (such as an attacker, or a natural disaster).

Alternatively, reactions may be caused by a phobia, which would suggest the mind had as some point learned to be fearful of something. However, this is so deeply ingrained, that logic, reason, and a measured response become impossible, and the instinctual physical reaction is overwhelming.

There are other involuntary responses associated with this system such as pupil dilation and sweating which can be seen in most animals when they deal with stress or imminent danger.

Another survival strategy would be to stand your ground when confronted with a threat to your survival. If there was an aggressive animal present and they were substantially larger than you, you may put up a fight. This could be to mask any sense of your own weaknesses. Or you may use your body language to threaten them so that they back down before it becomes necessary for you to use physical force to defend yourself. Should that occur, blood will rush towards your arms and hands ready for you carry out defensive or offensive manoeuvres in the form of punches, blocking manoeuvres, or restraining and immobilising the threat!

While it may seem simple for people to react spontaneously to a situation, what would you do if your primitive brain hasn't reacted to either fighting or fleeing? You experience the 'freeze' response - rooted to the spot, unable to run away.

This strategy will occur naturally when we feel we can't attack or escape from an assailant. When this happens, our 'consciously' thinking brain, steps out of the way for our primitive brains to take over. We are instinctively instructed to stop moving, shrink away from the danger, shut down bodily functions unnecessary for survival including digestion, circulation of blood - you get the picture. Basically, it means toning down your energy levels so as not to attract attention!

When faced with significant danger, we can flee, take fight or freeze. All three response systems are natural and part of our primitive survival instincts. When any situation is perceived as a threat, our primitive brains follow a certain set of criteria to protect us from the danger at hand. There is no room for negotiation to change your mind once it has decided, based on these instinctive principles (which could seem quite limiting, but is extremely efficient given the scope of its purpose, which is self-preservation)! The primitive brain prevents procrastination and denies us the opportunity to weigh up our options.

Once we accept the primitive physical brain as our security alert system, there are other important aspects to the physical state that affect us all, which can be helpful in our quest for understanding intuition.

1.b Physical Environmental States Of Energy

For intuition to function, we can set aside the primal physical states of instinctive reactions, as they are purely functional to survival. It is not something we can determine or evaluate.

The physical states of most interest to an intuitive, relate to your physical life balance, your world, your environment and how you decide to respond to it. Decision is the key factor here.

Environmental states of energy include your health, your personal environments, such as home, work, places of interest, sexuality. It relates to your relationships and interactions with other physical beings such as friends, family, colleagues, other professionals. It includes animals, foods and plants, hobbies, skills, and habits. In fact, anything that as a human being requires you to be a conscious, 'thinking' participant, in a physical world and has an impact on your life, is part of your physical environmental state of energy.

An example an intuitive might offer, is to 'tune in' to your home environment and the dynamics of those who live there. Whether you enjoy it there, feel safe and happy, wish to move, or need to make changes.

The same could be applied to work, hobbies, relationships recreation, etc.

2. Mental Intuition - conscious control

The mental realms are what we also know as the controlling awareness of the mind, and relates deeply to your logic, intellect, and habits. It has a stake in helping you to make decisions and evaluate situations. However, it is most useful to us when our survival is not under imminent threat and the primitive brain has no need to be triggered. Therefore, we can consider the mental realm as the conscious mind. It is the awakened state in which we can control outcomes.

Society, culture, politics, work, home, and many other areas are focussed on practical solutions that require a rational conscious approach. Our experiences, education and every thought are stored within areas of the brain and become triggered when necessary.

However, unlike the primitive brain, we have a level of control as to how it affects us. It offers an opportunity for us to work with our knowledge and intellect and make decisions. We have time here to consider and weigh up our options.

Consciously thinking is mostly a positive part of our nature and our mental processes. It means that we can function within the expectations of our families, friends, colleagues, careers, communities, and our own self-perception. Yet overthinking everything, can lead to a separation from our fundamental soul needs. We lack the sense of feeling something is in our best interests when we overthink it. We can become too focussed on different outcomes and guilty of procrastination. Relying on our thoughts alone to guide us can also lead to functioning habitually, or too much to please others.

If something is part of our experience, our learning, and beliefs, we tend to work mostly with the mental aspects. But we are more than our thoughts and beliefs. Many of us can become stuck in the mental state of overthinking everything and that can also lead to indecisiveness.

From the perspective of general survival, our mental agility can help us make decisions, when the situation is not as instinctive and urgent as the primitive threat. Yet the conscious mind also sends all thoughts and experiences, into the limitless mind of the subconscious for emotional processing and storage.

As an intuitive, the mental realms reference our knowledge, education, political alignment, beliefs, attitudes, logical thinking and more. The conscious/mental mind translates the rising subconscious messages and helps us to analyse them through our senses and dreams. The conscious mind also sends all thoughts and experiences into the limitless mind of the subconscious. Where they remain until stimulated another time.

3. Emotional Intuition - subconscious control

Thoughts and desires which we either do not know about or have been forgotten, play a very important role in our subconscious life.

The emotional/subconscious state is often referred to as the "hidden brain" as it influences our thoughts, feelings, and behaviour without us being instantly aware of it. In other words, our conscious mind can recognise that we sense a change, but we will have to analyse its basis, it to find a solution or understanding.

The subconscious mind has the capability of being triggered by experiences. It can turn negative situations, to unexpected positive ones and vice versa. What's more, our subconscious mind remembers more than we could ever imagine.

The word "subconscious" comes from under or below -- it may reference parts of your brain which you have never been conscious of before. The difficulty here is that we are only aware of a small percentage of the function of the brain at present.

The Subconscious/emotional realm includes all those thoughts and memories which you have forgotten or those which you may not be aware of - until something from the physical, mental, or superconscious state activates them.

The subconscious, receiving information from both the conscious and superconscious minds, is working

24/7. Every experience from the physical and the existential world, passes into to the subconscious.

When something arouses a memory or experience, it manifests through the senses of vision, symbol, colour, taste, emotion, smell, sound etc. These experiences are instantly available to the conscious and superconscious minds. We must work out why or what triggers it, to understand it. Accepting it as it is, is the experience of most of us, unless we need to analyse why we experienced what we did. It is what it is, too.

Dreams are also believed to originate from the subconscious mind.

It can depend on our intention which energy states, the subconscious communicates with. Both the conscious and superconscious are most likely to be simultaneously aware of any subconscious impressions.

As an intuitive, working with the emotional/subconscious mind is to uncover the senses at work - the feelings and how they play a part in our lives. It is to uncover the hopes, dreams, and the creativity of the soul. We discover the essence of the human personality here.

Indeed, negative experiences reside here too, but it's important as an intuitive, that we don't reactivate a wound we have yet to discover how to heal - we empower ourselves and others with our positive discoveries.

4. Spiritual Intuition - superconsciousness energy states

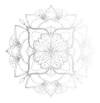

According to the Oxford English Dictionary, intuition is "the ability to understand or know something immediately, without conscious reasoning." In other words, it bypasses the mental and emotional aspect - the conscious and the subconscious.

Similar to the primitive brain, intuition arises almost spontaneously. Although it does not need a life threatening event to trigger it into action. For example, it is common for intuition to be active as we enter or withdraw from a meditation. Or when we rise early in the morning before the challenges of the day occupy our thoughts. In these moments many experience a moment of insight, clarity, or inspiration.

Intuition has brought us to where we are today more than we realise. You can control the conscious mind to an extent. The logic of your mental realm depends on your experience and knowledge. When applying logic to a decision or a thought - you have a choice to apply it from different perspectives.

Not so with genuine intuition. Your intuition is always there, nudging you and you can't decide how it makes you feel. It manifests within us and is different to the primitive and mental states of awareness. You can ignore it, but it doesn't disappear and remains in the shadows waiting for you to hear its whisper. You can forget something, but the subconscious won't.

The conscious mind may say 'take the new job' you were offered, when your intuition says 'no - it doesn't feel right.' What you decide will often come down to a combination of weighing up the pros and the cons with your feelings and applying rational thinking. But initially, you may feel flattered and think you should accept the new job regardless! It takes mental strength to say "I'll think about it and come back to you" when you are flattered or proud of your achievements.

The superconscious or spiritual realm is the gateway and space where we find the connection of the universal life force, the soul, the spirit, and the eternal nature of divine inspiration. It is the meeting place for your higher self and the universal consciousness. It is where the consciousness of our loved ones who have passed can connect with us. The function of the superconscious is to be connected to wisdom, inspiration, spiritual experiences, new ideas and happiness. It is where soul meets spirit, and the wisdom and presence of all spiritual consciousness resides.

As an intuitive, the superconscious mind is exciting! It's where we can access the energy of the soul, receive divine guidance, connect with the spiritual realms, discover wisdom, and experience the power of the universal life force.

In the superconscious state we may receive channelled information - the wisdom and knowledge of other great minds. We reconnect to the collective consciousness.

The superconscious state invites us to sense natural energy, pure emotion, and divine inspiration. It is the gateway to the soul, the spirit, and the afterlife, if we choose to explore.

In summary, the four major states of energy are **physical, mental, emotional, and spiritual.** They all offer us tremendous scope to survive, thrive, inspire, communicate, and adapt. Finding the balance and the trust is trickier, but potentially possible when we are aware of them.

In practice, people and situations can be evaluated by these four interactive states. As an intuitive psychic, (once you know how to connect and attune to the energy of a person or situation) you may systematically look at each aspect as **physical, mental, emotional, and spiritual** - to achieve an overall holistic perspective.

13

YOUR SUPER COMPUTER BRAIN

Our greatest resource that we rely upon, is the powerhouse between our ears - our brain! It has a vital role in processing intuitive information. It's a complex subject and so much is yet to be discovered about the relationship between intuition and the brain.

The practice of the four intuitive energy states of physical, mental, emotional, and spiritual are constructive to working with intuition. Most of us are not living with an equal balance of them. We tend to go through our daily lives functioning without considering the harmony of our own energy, until there is a problem. While this is ongoing, our fluctuating brain patterns are in a state of processing for us.

So much of the brain and its functions are yet to be known. What we do know is fascinating and in considering this knowledge, we may accept the interplay between a physical and a spiritual system.

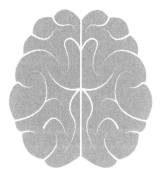 In layman's terms, the brain is divided into two major halves (hemispheres). These hemispheres are connected by a structure known as the corpus callosum, which are a

bundle of communicating
nerve fibres.

The corpus callosum acts as a bridge between the two hemispheres and structurally holds it all together, encased in the skull. It also means that communication between the two halves can flow back and forth easily.

The corpus callosum sends and receives physical, chemical, electrical impulses and stimuli. It is a human, primary information superhighway!

This flow of information is important, because we think that specific areas of the brain store different but essential information. Yet, something arising in one part, profoundly affects another area.

For example: your visual part of the brain may register an image. However, another area of the brain will process it by connecting to knowledge, language, memories, associations, emotions etc. Your response to this may determine how you think, act, or intuitively express yourself.

The left side of the brain was often associated with logic, reasoning, mathematics, language, speech, decision making and what we think of as being pragmatic. Whilst former theories believed the right side only included associations with feelings, colours, symbols, creativity, art, and intuition.

Everything is interconnected and there is an interdependence between the two halves. When one half is unreachable or damaged, we function differently and the brain attempts to reroute its data when blocked.

Despite its popularity, the left-brain, right-brain theory is not supported by current scientific evidence. Studies using functional magnetic resonance imaging (fMRI) have shown that both hemispheres of the brain are actively engaged in almost all cognitive tasks. While it is true that some tasks may activate certain regions more than others, these areas are not exclusively confined to one hemisphere.

Moreover, the idea that a person can be classified as left-brained or right-brained is an oversimplification that ignores the complex and dynamic nature of the human brain. The brain is a highly interconnected organ, with both hemispheres constantly communicating.

Embracing a whole-brain approach to cognition acknowledges the intricate interplay between the left and right hemispheres. Rather than viewing cognitive functions as isolated within a single hemisphere, the whole-brain perspective appreciates the synergistic relationship between the two. This approach can have significant implications for education, mental health, personal development and intuition.

For instance, in education, adopting a whole-brain approach can lead to more balanced and inclusive teaching methods that cater to diverse learning styles. Similarly, in mental health, understanding that the brain functions as an integrated unit can help create more effective treatments and interventions that target the entire brain, rather than just one hemisphere.

The whole-brain approach's impact on intuition can be better appreciated by acknowledging the dynamic interplay between various brain regions and their roles in intuitive processes, - even when we don't have full comprehension of neuroscience.

Intuition, often considered a product of the right hemisphere, is most likely a result of the entire brain's intricate network, with both hemispheres working together in a coordinated manner. This could help us in many sphere's of functioning.

- Integration of Information: Intuition is often thought of as the ability to make accurate judgments or decisions without relying on conscious reasoning. A whole-brain approach suggests that intuition arises from the integration of information from various brain regions, including those responsible for emotions, memory, and sensory processing. This integration enables individuals to rapidly process and synthesise information, resulting in intuitive insights.

- Enhanced Learning and Decision-Making: Embracing the whole-brain approach can help individuals become more attuned to their intuitive abilities by recognising the importance of both analytical and creative thinking. By combining logical reasoning with intuitive insights, people can make more informed decisions and improve their learning experiences. This approach can be particularly beneficial in situations where rapid decision-making is required or where information is incomplete or ambiguous.

- Personal Development and Self-Awareness: Developing a greater understanding of the whole-brain approach can lead to increased self-awareness and personal growth. By recognising that intuition is a result of complex brain interactions, individuals can

work on nurturing their intuitive abilities
through practices like mindfulness,
meditation, or engaging in activities that
challenge and stimulate their cognitive
processes.

- Professional Applications: In professional
settings, a whole-brain approach to intuition
can lead to improved problem-solving,
decision-making, and innovation. By
acknowledging the importance of intuition
and encouraging the integration of both
logical and intuitive thinking, organisations
can foster a culture that values diverse
perspectives and supports creative solutions
to complex challenges.

The comprehensive approach towards developing
intuition highlights the significant interrelationship
between various regions of the brain and cognitive
abilities.

The left-brain, right-brain theory, while popular and
influential, has been debunked by contemporary
neuroscience.

The neuroanatomist Jill Bolte Taylor, shares her own
personal experience in her book 'My Stroke of
Insight,'[1] and she is featured on YouTube, relating to

when one hemisphere of her brain became severely damaged, her experiences and recovery.

At the age of 37, she suffered a devastating stroke in the left brain. She wasn't expected to survive, but she did, and she had to re-learn every skill such as speech, reading, writing, mathematics, science and walking, from the functioning of her undamaged right brained hemisphere.

In her book she writes about the incredible insights and existential experiences she encountered during her recovery and rehabilitation. Without the balance of the two healthy brain's hemispheres, she experienced life in recovery, mostly in a creative, emotional mental space. Now recovered to a high functioning state again, she now includes in her daily life an essential need to explore her creative expression, through art.

Her left brain has not returned to its pre-stroke condition, but somehow, she has bypassed or re-routed the neurological instructions to manage everyday functioning and a good standard of life and work again.

The human brain is constantly communicating with our senses, processing every emotion, image, scent, taste, and thought. This internal dialogue can have a profound impact on our physical wellbeing. In moments of intense emotional stress, the brain may send chemical signals to the body, triggering a range of physical responses such as accelerated heart rate, increased sweating, and narrowed blood vessels.

The way these signals manifest will vary from person to person, as each individual's response to stress is unique. Nonetheless, paying attention to these bodily cues can provide valuable insight into our intuitive experiences. By remaining aware of how our emotions and thoughts affect our physical state, we can cultivate greater self-awareness and take more intentional actions to maintain our wellbeing

The intricate interplay between our physical, mental, emotional, and spiritual states is truly remarkable! It's clear that just as our brains can rewire and reroute themselves, we can tap into multiple sources of insight, creativity, and wisdom through our intuition. Remember, the possibilities for growth and transformation are endless when we embrace the profound connection between our brain, mind, body, heart, and soul.

Every related image, idea, colour, and scent (smell is the strongest and most impressionable of the five senses when it comes to memory) triggers a response in our minds - activates an area of the brain and the body will respond.

Whilst a good intuitive does not need training in neuroscience or cognitive psychology, a respectful nod and mindfulness for the complexities, is helpful.

The brain can also reactivate memories and associations which in turn either correlate or conflict with the present moment or context. This may result in experiencing strong emotions and physical symptoms. If you have ever awoken from a vivid dream about a loved one who has passed, you will know how this feels. It can start the day overwhelmed by emotion and reduce you to tears.

Such a domino effect induces more change for equilibrium to be sought, between what we see, know and what we feel on both a physical, mental, emotional, and spiritual level. It's only when things balance out, that no further change is required, and we feel in harmony. Until the next idea or sensory event!

It's complex - we are complex, but it's natural and underpins the belief that everything is connected. It is the law of cause and effect in action.

The self-awareness of our physical, mental, emotional, and spiritual experiences, ensure that as an intuitive, you have many clues to consider when working with your intuition.

The greatest of intuitive experiences relate to us personally. The amazing relationship between the four energy states is within your own grasp to explore, analyse or detach from. You are the creator of your intuitive experiences.

How you experience the big four energy states, is a subjective personal journey of perception, sight, sound, taste, scent, emotion, sensation, instinct, memory and more. Acknowledging the vital role of the super computer brain in the process, ensures we recognise how complex and spectacular intuition is.

1. My Stroke of Insight by Jill Bolte Taylor **Ph.D.**
   ASIN: B002V092B0
   Publisher: Hodder & Stoughton (19 Mar. 2009)

14

YOUR MIND, BODY & SOUL IS TALKING TO YOU

Intuition is my soul speaking,
And I listen with my heart.
It's the voice of my higher self,
Guiding me to my true north.
I trust my intuition,
And follow its lead.

The link between our physical and mental health is globally accepted. Stress accounts for causing or exacerbating many physical problems, including:

- headaches

- digestive issues

- heart attacks

- high blood pressure

- respiratory symptoms

- panic attacks

- weakened immune system

- skin disorders

- sleep disruption

There is also research that suggests an imbalance between the mind and body can create the perfect storm for cancer cells to proliferate and metastasise. A large study published in 2016, concluded that anxiety increased the risk of men dying of cancer by 2.15 times higher than the average.[1]

The reverse is also true and improving our mental health has a positive effect on our physical wellbeing.

In conversation we may describe our negative emotions relating to the body, such as:

- feeling kicked in the gut or teeth

- stabbed in the heart, or the back.

- making you flesh crawl

- a sight for sore eyes

Clearly, it is recognised that we may describe a physical experience, to explain how we feel emotionally.

An intuitive, relies upon these feelings as part of their skillset too.

It helps us if we can consciously make time to feel balance with the mind, the body, and the soul. Intuition works best for us when we are living in a state of harmony.

The following two chapters are dedicated to creating balance and working with your body as an intuitive compass.

---

1. https://www.livescience.com/56195-anxiety-cancer-men.html

15

BALANCE EXERCISE

There is a balance to be found
Between the mind, body and soul
And when we find that perfect harmony
We are whole and complete
Ready to take on whatever life throws our way

Balance Exercise:

- Turn off any phones and remove any distractions and have a glass of water nearby?
- You are making valuable time for yourself.
- Relax into a comfortable chair.
- Close your eyes.
- And when ready focus on your breathing.
- Be aware of the rise and fall of the chest.
- Take this a little deeper now and imagining that with each inhalation.
- Your breath is entering through your solar plexus.
- Keep your focus here for a few more moments, imagine that in your head are thousands of thoughts and visualise them represented as a thick, golden liquid, sinking down through your body as it reaches the soles of your feet, you feel roots burrowing down into the floor.
- The roots continue down into the soil past the rock layers and the tips of the roots begin to glow with the warmth from the Earth's golden core. You let the thoughts in the golden liquid flow into the earth's core and leave them here.

- You begin to draw up the golden light of the earth, through your root system.
- It reaches your feet and merges with the thoughts you placed there.
- Now, draw the earth's golden light through your body.
- Visualise it filling your feet legs trunk chest arms, neck, head, and right to the crown of you.
- As you sit filled with the earth's light.
- Now, imagine a pure white ray of light entering your crown.
- It is a cleansing spiritual light.
- Let it flow through you.
- Send with your mind, light down through your body, and let reach the roots.
- The light travels down further towards the earth's core, as you sit, you are filled from below with the energy of mother earth and from above the power of spirit.
- Now for a few minutes and then go back to focusing on breathing through the solar plexus.
- It's time to draw this exercise to a close.
- Let the earth energy from your solar plexus drop back down through the root system to mother earth as it leaves your body.

- Let your light of spirit power travel back up to your crown and leave your body.
- Take a couple of deep breaths and some sips of water to ground yourself

16

THE INTUITIVE BODY SCAN: EXERCISE

When you're feeling lost and unsure,
Trust your gut, it will guide you for sure.
It knows what's best for you,
So trust it and see what you can do.
Believe in yourself

Intuitive Body Scan: A Path To Wholeness

The human body is a magnificent and complex organism that is constantly sending us signals. These signals contain important information about our physical, mental, emotional, and spiritual well-being. Unfortunately, in our fast-paced, modern lives, we often overlook these messages, leading to imbalances and a disconnection from our true selves.

The intuitive body scan is a powerful technique that can help you reconnect with your body, enhance your self-awareness, and promote healing and well-being. This chapter will explore the theory behind the intuitive body scan, provide step-by-step guidance on how to practice it, and discuss the many benefits of incorporating this technique into your daily life.

The Theory Behind the Intuitive Body Scan

The intuitive body scan is based on the belief that our bodies are not only physical entities but also energetic systems, interconnected with our minds, emotions, and spirits. When we notice the sensations and energy within our bodies, we can gain valuable insights into our overall health and wellbeing.

This technique encourages a deep level of self-awareness, promoting the understanding that our physical, mental, emotional, and spiritual aspects are all connected. By tuning into these different dimensions, we can identify areas that need attention and care, ultimately fostering a greater sense of balance and wholeness.

The Benefits of the Intuitive Body Scan

By incorporating the intuitive body scan into your daily life, you can experience a multitude of benefits, including:

• Enhanced self-awareness: The intuitive body scan helps you become more in tune with your body's signals, promoting a deeper understanding of your physical, mental, emotional, and spiritual needs.

• Reduced stress and anxiety: By tuning into your body's sensations and releasing tension, you can effectively lower your stress and anxiety levels.

• Improved physical health: By identifying areas of discomfort and tension in your body, you can take steps to address these issues and improve your overall health.

• Emotional healing: The practice of observing and acknowledging your emotions without judgment can foster emotional healing and growth.

• Spiritual growth: By connecting with your spiritual aspect during the intuitive body scan, you can deepen your sense of purpose, inner wisdom, and interconnectedness.

The intuitive body scan is a powerful tool for fostering self-awareness and promoting healing on multiple levels.

How to Practice the Intuitive Body Scan

To begin your intuitive body scan, find a comfortable and quiet place where you can sit or lie down undisturbed. Close your eyes, and take several deep, slow breaths to centre yourself and quiet your mind.

A. Physical Awareness: Starting at the top of your head, slowly bring your awareness to each part of your body, one at a time. As you slowly move through your body, notice any sensations or discomfort, cold, warmth, pressure you may be experiencing. Do not judge or analyse these sensations, simply observe, and acknowledge them.

B. Mental Awareness: Rescan your body, pay attention to any thoughts or mental images that arise. Observe these thoughts without judgment or attachment, allowing them to flow through your mind like clouds passing through the sky.

C. Emotional Awareness: Rescan again for emotion. You may notice emotions that are present within you. Again, simply observe and acknowledge these emotions without judgment or attachment. Allow yourself to feel the emotions fully, embracing their presence as part of your experience.

D. Spiritual Awareness: Finally, as you complete your scan, turn your attention to your spiritual aspect. This may involve connecting with your inner wisdom, your intuition, or a higher power. Focus on the sensations of peace, love, and interconnectedness that you experience as you tap into this spiritual dimension.

.

17

THE INTUITIVE HEART

The Intelligence of Heart Coherence and its Relationship with Intuition

The human heart has long been associated with emotions, intuition, and wisdom in various cultures and traditions. As we delve deeper into the realm of heart intelligence, we discover that the heart's role in our cognitive processes and emotional well-being is more profound than previously understood. The concept of heart coherence, explored extensively by the HeartMath Institute,[1] has emerged as a key element in understanding this hidden intelligence and its relationship with intuition.

The Science of Heart Coherence

Heart coherence refers to the harmonious functioning of the heart, brain, and nervous system. This state is characterised by increased heart rate variability (HRV), which is the natural fluctuation in time between successive heartbeats. Higher HRV is associated with improved physical and mental health, emotional regulation, and cognitive performance.

The HeartMath Institute has developed several techniques and technologies to facilitate the achievement of a coherent state, which involves generating feelings of appreciation, love, or compassion. These positive emotions can help shift the autonomic nervous system from the stress-induced "fight or flight" response to a more balanced "rest and digest" state.

Heart-Brain Communication

The heart and brain communicate with each other through neural, hormonal, and electromagnetic pathways. Research at the HeartMath Institute has revealed that the heart's electromagnetic field can be detected several feet away from the body and can influence the brainwaves of nearby individuals. This suggests that our emotions not only affect our own well-being but also have the potential to affect those around us.

The heart sends more information to the brain than the brain sends to the heart, highlighting the heart's role in influencing our emotional experiences and cognitive processes. When the heart's rhythmic patterns are coherent, the signals sent to the brain facilitate cortical functioning, promoting mental clarity and emotional stability.

Intuition and the Heart's Intelligence

Intuition, often described as a gut feeling or inner knowing, is a powerful form of nonverbal communication that transcends conscious reasoning. HeartMath's research has shown that the heart plays a pivotal role in processing and conveying intuitive information.

In a series of experiments, participants were exposed to emotionally arousing images. Both the heart and the brain responded to the images before they were consciously perceived. The heart, however, responded more quickly, showing that it may be the first organ to receive and process intuitive information.

This research suggests that heart coherence may enhance our intuitive abilities by facilitating the heart's capacity to access and transmit intuitive information. When we are in a coherent state, our cognitive and emotional systems function harmoniously, allowing us to tap into our inner wisdom more effectively.

Harnessing Heart Coherence for Intuitive Living

Developing heart coherence and nurturing our intuitive abilities can have a transformative impact on our lives. By cultivating practices that promote heart coherence, we can foster a deeper connection with our intuition, enabling us to make wiser decisions, build more meaningful relationships, and navigate life's challenges with grace and resilience.

Some practical steps for achieving heart coherence include:

- Practice heart-focused breathing: Inhale and exhale slowly and deeply, focusing on the area around your heart. This simple technique can help to balance the autonomic nervous system and induce a coherent state.
- Cultivate positive emotions: Engage in activities that bring you joy, practice gratitude, and generate feelings of compassion for yourself and others.
- Use HeartMath tools and techniques: The HeartMath Institute offers a range of resources, including the emWave and Inner Balance technologies, to help individuals achieve and maintain heart coherence.
- By integrating heart coherence practices into our daily lives, we can unlock the potential of

our heart's intelligence and strengthen our intuitive abilities.

---

1. www.heartmath.org

PART 3: WORKING WITH INTUITIVE ENERGY SYSTEMS

18

THE ENERGETIC CHAKRA SYSTEM

The word "chakra" is derived from the Sanskrit word for "wheel." Ancient practitioners of eastern medicine believed that seven major points on each person's body, have been designated as being particularly sensitive gates, or stations. These chakras, process and transport life force energy, between the root of the body, connecting our physicality to the crown of the head, and connecting our spiritual aspects to the universe.

The chakras are those stations and are a complex, ancient energy system prevalent in India, as far as the earliest, historical references show. They were first discovered in the Vedas, which are ancient sacred texts of spiritual knowledge, considered by most scholars to date from 1500–1200 bce. Today the importance of the chakras has stood the test of time and scientific advancements, and are still relevant today, in many intuitive, healing and yogic practices.

There are seven major chakras (wheel centres) in the body, but there are other minor chakras too. These are also found in all traditions of eastern medicine and Buddhism. We will focus on the seven major chakras and how we can work with them through intuition.

Each chakra is located within the body and each one has an effect on the others. Linking them all is a network of energetic channels called meridians. Meridians transport energy back and forth and between them all. When one chakra is depleting, the others compensate by delivering more energy through the channels. However, this can create an imbalance and the results can be felt by a person and also sensed by an intuitive. A little knowledge of the chakra system can yield a lot of intuitive information.

The seven major chakras are positioned from the base of the spine to the crown of the head in a straight line. Each chakra rotates in a spinning motion. The slowest rotation is the base chakra and the fastest the crown chakra. If you work from the ground up, the spinning speed indicates the vibratory nature of each chakra, with the higher vibration at the crown having the fastest revolutions and relating to the spiritual dimensions. Whilst the root chakra closest to the earth and physical environment, being the slowest.

Chakra locations, their symbols and direction of rotation

Whilst we can number each chakra, they do have a Sanskrit name and a modern name. See table below:[1]

Position	Colour	Modern Name	Sanskrit Name
1	Red	Root	Muladhara
2	Orange	Sacral	Svadhishthana
3	Yellow	Solar Plexus	Manipura
4	Green or Pink	Heart	Anahata
5	Blue	Throat	Vishuddha
6	Indigo	Third Eye	Ajna
7	Magenta or White	Crown	Sahastrara

Chakra Names

Each of the chakras are represented by one of seven unique symbols, which correspond to the meaning and essence of each chakra's purpose. All the symbols incorporate a powerful circle – a universal design used for many thousands of years to symbolise connection and unity with ourselves, other beings and a higher spiritual purpose.

Every chakra symbol also represents the lotus flower, and has a specific number of lotus flower petals. The more petals attached to the chakra symbol, the higher the frequency of energy that the chakra is attuned to. For example: The base chakras have fewer petals and lower frequencies of energy than the crown chakra with its 1000 petals and the highest frequency.

If that wasn't enough information about each chakra, then we have to add their unique colour. Every chakra colour has a frequency range and each chakra a frequency, which corresponds to a system of the body that matches the colour frequency. It is all connected.

As referenced before, each chakra corresponds to systems of the body. We discover that they also have a physical, emotional and mental relationship. In this handy guide on the next page, we can also consider what an imbalance reveals. To view or print the full sized version, the download link is within the endnotes.

ENERGY CENTRE (CHAKRA)	PHYSICAL	EMOTIONAL	MENTAL	IMBALANCE	COLOUR
ROOT	Joints and bones, intestines, stamina, physical energy	Trust, security and survival, foundations.	Groundedness, abundance, letting go, contentedness	Feels lacking security, community, feels disconnected, food issues, 'spacey'	Red
SACRAL	Bladder, lower back, reproductive system, fluid functions.	Passion, creativity, desire, attraction, isolation, guilt, fear, isolation.	Wisdom creation, relationships, sexuality.	Creative balance, lower back pain, fertility, passion, emotional & sex related stability	Orange
SOLAR PLEXUS	Stomach, digestion, gall bladder, pancreas, liver, nervous system	Joy, anger, fear, self-belief, ego, willpower, personal power, seat of emotion	Intention, focus, Intelligence, manifestation, ambition, critical/defensive	Control issues, fatigue, stomach ulcers, anxiety, hyper-sensitivity, feeling powerless	Yellow
HEART	Lungs, circulation, arms, hands, fingers, ribs, immune system	Self-love, love of all life and others, forgiveness, compassion, trust, empathy, vulnerability	Self-love, fear, isolation, balanced, self-sufficient, independence/co-dependence	Lack of self love, cardiac/lung problems, trust issues, depression, fear, loneliness	Green &/or Pink
THROAT	Breathing, throat, jaw, lower neck, vocal chords, thyroid, lungs	Sharing, creative expression, decision making, communication	Innovation, self-expression, memories of love and fear, communication	Misguidance, creative blocks, colds, flu, sore throats	Blue
THIRD EYE	Sinuses, eyes, nose, upper neck, pituitary gland, brain	Intuition, inspiration, truth, dreams, perception	Wisdom, insight, intellect, intuition, mind power	Headaches, insomnia, vertigo, memory problems, emotional breakdown	Indigo
CROWN	Skin, brain, skull, pineal gland, nervous system	Peace, clarity, consciousness, divine healing and energy	Higher self-perception, divine connection, totality of all chakras	Idealism, confusion, spiritual obsession, atheism, depression, irrational	Magenta

Medical intuition chart of the chakras

We haven't stopped yet - each chakra also has a unique sound that can be chanted too! Chanting each chakra is believed to place a vibration and intention, which maintains, or restores its optimum frequency for good health.

ROOT	LAM
SACRAL	VAM
SOLAR PLEXUS	RAM
HEART	YAM
THROAT	HAM
THRID EYE	OM
CROWN	OM or SILENCE

Chakra Sound Chants

The subject of the chakra system is vast and to study it fully would take many books, courses, individual and group practice. For our purposes as intuitives, we need at least a basic knowledge to begin and this starts with knowing:

- where they are located
- their common names

- colours
- a basic understanding of what each chakra broadly represents.

All the information is found within the intuition chart and additional diagrams which can be downloaded from the link in the endnotes and from the resources section.

An 'in - depth' study of the chakras is ideal, should the intuitive wish to deepen their knowledge of this ancient, yet significant energy system. However, a great starting point or revision, is to begin with learning to meditate on each chakra yourself. This will ensure self knowledge and is a memorable experience, that will assist with learning the main points of the chakras.

You will truly know the significance of the chakra system, if you learn from yourself first and then sensing the chakra system with your intuition will serve you well.

In the next chapter, there are some tips on meditation and a link to download a recording of a guided exercise focussing on each chakra and includes affirmations.

---

1. https://developingspirit.com/course-detail/chakra-power-exercise/1448

19

CHAKRA MEDITATION: EXERCISE

A meditation routine can provide us with peace, gratitude, calm, healing, development of intuition or any other number of benefits. Importantly, you do not need any kind of spiritual practice or belief for this technique to work.

If you are willing to commit to the process, I can promise you that you will see amazing results.Many of us live in a fast paced world and it is important to find techniques and exercises to help ground our energy and reconnect with who we really are. We often turn to meditation as a way to remember how to be in the moment.

It is important to have everything ready before starting a meditation.

Tips For Meditation

- Prepare, so you have a clear mind and positive experience with no interruptions. It doesn't need to take long, but an intention and a few practical tips as set out below will help.
- Choose the time you feel most relaxed with.
- It can be any time during daytime or in the evening, although avoid being overly tired when meditating.
- Don't meditate while being distracted or rushed. Instead, you should focus on one thing at a time.
- Duration shouldn't be the primary focus, but rather a consistency.
- Find yourself a spot where you can be comfortable.
- Make sure to adjust the room temperature to your comfort if you are inside.
- You should find a spot where you feel comfortable and uninterrupted.
- You can also use music, relaxing music if it helps.
- Mastering meditation techniques takes some practice, but you'll get there soon.

- Since there is no shortcut to success, you should make the most of each experience by being consistent.
- If you want to get anything out of meditation, you need to make it a regular part of your life

Download you FREE guided chakra meditation & charts[1]

1. https://developingspirit.com/course-detail/chakra-power-exercise/1448

20

THE AURIC FIELD

An auric field is a subtle electro - magnetic energy field that constantly surrounds us. It is commonly referred to as, 'the aura.'

In its simplest form, it can be considered a natural energy field that originates from the physical body and extends beyond it. The aura is considered as a subtle reflection of the state of our mind, body, soul, and our spirit. Although it may be affected by environmental factors too.

This may happen in areas of high radio frequencies, microwaves, highly magnetic thunderstorms etc. Some people are highly sensitive to electro-magnetic energy, and feel unwell or stressed when their body is closely subjected to it. In such cases, we could expect that their human auras reflect this stress.

The auric field represents the balance within and around every living creature and regulates communication between different parts of an organism's body. It is not exclusive to humans and everything that has an energy field, has an electro - magnetic aura too.

There is a lot of controversy surrounding the human aura. Some people believe that the human aura is simply a result of an individual's consciousness and spirit, while others believe it to be a purely physical phenomenon. Many believe it to be a combination of both the consciousness, spirit, soul and the physical state.

Since the human aura also reflects one's emotional state, it can be used as a tool to assess someone's emotional condition before meeting them face-to-face. The human aura which emanates from every living organism on this planet, is amplified by contact with other beings, but it can also be weakened by intense emotions like fear, anger, and sadness. When content and in good health, the aura is expansive and the colours are brightest. When sad, angry or unwell, the auric filed is close to the body and tends to be dulled.

The auric energy field is so subtle that for most of us, it is invisible to the naked eye. Yet, it is detectable by our senses and even by our intuition. It is the natural electro-magnetic field of the human body.

Those who can see an aura tend to do so by clairvoyance. Mostly they will view within the mind, although some may see it objectively as a physical image. Yet this is still a clairvoyant experience as the image will be unique to them and unseen by most others. Even when more than one person can clairvoyantly see the aura so physically objectively, interpretations will be unique to the eye and intuition of the beholder.

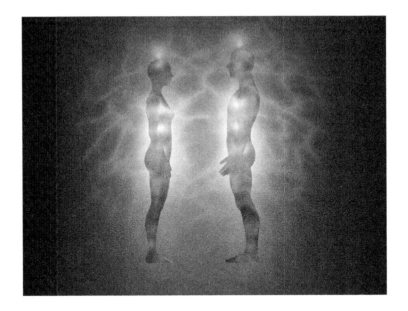

We do know that although interpreting the aura can be subjective and controversial to some, it can actually be photographed. This type of photography was pioneered by the invention of the Kirlian camera. Simply put, it is a device that uses electromagnetic radiation to capture images. Unlike traditional cameras that use light waves to create an image on film or electronic sensors, a Kirlian camera collects energy emitted by objects. Kirlian cameras for human use, involves the subject placing a hand on an metal plate. This plate then reconstructs the image, using electromagnetic fields.

This technology was pioneered by Dr. Semyon Kirlian in the 1950s. It has since been used by scientists and photographers to capture images of living organisms, objects with unusual properties, and even extraterrestrial objects.

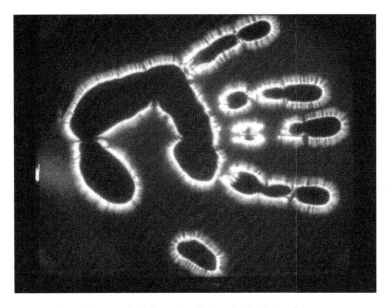

Kirlian photograph of the palm of a hand. The light of the aura is shown around the physical form.

In one famous Kirlian photograph, the aura of a leaf remained in situ after it had been picked and discarded. This demonstrated that life force is detectable for some time, even when the physical no longer remains present. This may explain why we intuitively sense things we cannot always see.

On one occasion, I believe I experienced this phenomena with another person's aura. I had been away on a working trip to Greece and my flight landed at Manchester airport. At the time I lived in York, so it was short walk to the train platform and a two hour direct train ride home.

As I entered the arrivals hall, I was struck with an intense feeling that my friend Kate was waiting for me. This had not been arranged and I don't believe she knew what flight I was on. I couldn't see her, but the feeling was so strong that she was there. It was so intense that I didn't go to the train station immediately. Instead I bought a coffee and sat down whilst I looked around for her.

I tried phoning her but there was no answer. I just couldn't shake the feeling that Kate was there. After a while, I decided it was time to get the train and so I did.

That evening Kate finally answered my many phone messages. She confirmed that as a surprise, she had come to the arrivals hall to meet me from my flight. The airport was very busy that day and we missed each other. Kate had gone home just before I got my airport coffee. As I was sat drinking it she was no longer in the building, yet I was convinced I would turn around and she would be there in person.

Energetically, she left her impression and I was sensing it very strongly.

Modern aura cameras and computer software attempt to photograph the aura in a similar fashion and produce a polaroid photo of a person with more colour enhancements. The subject places a hand on a sensitive metal plate again and the signals recorded, match pre - programmed colour frequencies. In this scenario, the photo is of the person and not the hand. The hand allows the energy frequencies to be read and interpreted. The colours selected are then impressed on the photo and often, the subject will receive an intuitive colour reading, based on the results.

For many of us, we sense the aura and we often do this without realising or at least being conscious of what is happening.

What fascinates us, is that intuition is more than a notion or a personal belief. It can be interwoven with an energetic field when something is physically absent.

21

SEEING THE AURA: EXERCISE 7

Seeing The Aura Exercise

Try the following exercise with another person.

- Place your subject so that they are standing with their back to a wall, with a gap of approximately 6 inches.
- Ensure the wall is a plain surface, and is of a light neutral colour.
- Ask them to close their eyes and take some relaxing breaths.
- Stand approximately 10 feet away from them and focus on the tip of their nose for half a minute.

- Soften your gaze and after you have relaxed your eyes notice any subtle changes in the outline of the body of your subject.
- Try doing this a few times a day if you can, until you can distinguish the outline.

The primary auric outline closest to the body, may be seen as a white light and extends to a few centimetres.

Over time and with practice, you many begin to see flares, tints, shades of colour emerging around the body outline.

If you look too intensely, you may find it difficult to see the first auric layer. Simply relax your gaze and use your peripheral vision.

22

INTUITING THE AURA: EXERCISE

The Intuitive Visual Aura is another method for experiencing the aura. This will require your intuition, clairvoyance and creativity.

This method uses your intuition and is useful for both in person assessment and when the subject is not with you. It also requires psychic skills of clairvoyance and clairsentience.

A template of the outline of a body and some coloured pencils or paints are required. If you prefer, you may create your own template, scan, print or trace the outline included in this chapter.

Method:

1. With your template and colours ready, take few conscious breaths and close your eyes.
2. With your mind, ask for the intention to be shown the colours of the aura for your subject and spend a few moments thinking about the person.
3. In your third eye recreate the image of their body outline. (we need this to be an outline, as if you start imagining them in human form, clothed and with all the patterns and colours of what they wear, it may influence your mind)

4. Putting all thoughts about colours and chakras aside, now invite the image in your mind to show you colours around and within the body. Don't worry if you think you are imagining it - let your intuition guide you. Let it simply arise. Sit with this for a minute or two and commit as much of what you see to memory

5. Open your eyes and with your colours, fill the blank body outline picture, with where you saw all the colours.

If this method works for you, it can also form the basis of a colour reading, as well as a useful guide for a colour healing session.

On the next page is a basic body outline template you can copy.

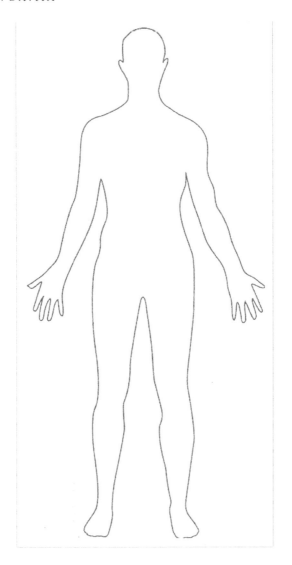

Analysis

Once you have your image of the colours there are a number of areas you can work with. The following is a guide to analysing your colour experiment.

1. What are you first impressions and your feelings about the results?
2. How does this make you feel about their energy states in the physical, emotional, mental and spiritual aspects?
3. Referring to the colour quick reference guides, is there balance? If not, where does balance need to be restored?
4. Areas that appear dark or too bright may need more tints, or complementary colours for balance
5. Do you see a balance of cool or warm colours? If too cool or warm again add the complement
6. Is there one colour that dominates or overpowers? Add in new colours?
7. Consider the position of the chakras and if their colours appear to overwhelm another chakra. For example, if you have a lot of red over the heart area, it could be interpreted as someone who is too emotionally attached to materialism or physical power.

As you become more familiar with the energy centres, the states of energy and the colours, more will be revealed to you. It just takes practice and colour consciousness.

Also, if you are confident with your clairvoyance, you can try without the plain outline and bring a realistic image of the person to your mind, inviting the colours to show themselves. If you start to feel your conscious influence is too great - return to the plain outline. Be as expressive as your inspiration guides you.

Experienced intuitives may work with eyes open and the ability to see the colours clairvoyantly whilst simultaneously describing your findings. Others may prefer to close their eyes. All methods can work, so play around with them and with practice the ability to see aura colours could develop.

Important note: If your knowledge of the chakras is quite confident, you may be tempted to see the colours in the aura of a person, as being in the same area as their corresponding chakra. Free your mind and let the colours evolve wherever you see them and trust. Let your intuition be your guide.

23

PSYCHOMETRY - THE ART OF SENSING THROUGH OBJECTS

Psychometry - The Art of Sensing Through Objects

Psychometry, also known as token-object reading, is a fascinating psychic skill that allows individuals to perceive information about a person or event by touching or holding an object related to them. As you do this, you can connect intuitively and discover information.

There is a theory that everything we touch, or everything that exists has an energy signature. This signature can change depending upon the influences that either touch it, or are present within its field of energy, such as environments, emotions and atmospheric conditions.

If we take the example of a brand new wedding ring in a shop window, it has only come into contact with the manufacturers, the shop workers and briefly members of the public who may have tried it on. There will be natural energies within the ring from the metals, but significant changes of emotion and experience have not played a large role in its existence.

Compare this to an antique wedding ring that has been passed down the family generations. Such a wedding ring has had close contact throughout the lives of others. It has been worn close to the body and the people who wore it, will have experienced many events in their lives. Their energy will have changed over time and the ring will have been present during this. Its original energy fingerprint would have changed. Also, it may have been resized several times and have some wear and tear.

A good psychometrist, by holding one of these rings, will intuitively read the energy and share their impressions. It's all about the energy and the intuitive ability.

Benefits of Psychometry

The practice of psychometry offers numerous benefits, making it a valuable tool for intuitive readers and investigators alike. By tapping into the energy and history of an object, a psychometrist can uncover information that might otherwise remain hidden. Some of the benefits of psychometry include:

1. Gaining insight into the history of an object or its owner, which can be especially useful when examining antiques or family heirlooms.

2. Uncovering lost or forgotten memories by connecting with personal items, which can be particularly helpful in therapy or healing work.

3. Assisting in criminal investigations by providing intuitive insights into evidence or belongings of a suspect or victim.

4. Enhancing psychic abilities by developing the skill of tuning into the energy of objects, which can strengthen other psychic senses such as clairvoyance and clairsentience.

History and Research

The term "psychometry" was first coined in the 19th century by American physician and professor Joseph R. Buchanan. He conducted experiments in which he discovered that some individuals could sense information about a person or event by touching objects related to them. This early research laid the foundation for further exploration into the field of psychometry.

Throughout the years, many psychical researchers have studied psychometry and its potential applications. Some of these studies have included controlled experiments, while others have involved spontaneous cases reported by psychometrists themselves. Although not all research findings have been conclusive, many suggest that psychometry is a genuine psychic phenomenon worthy of further study.

Famous Psychometrists

Several well-known psychometrists have gained recognition for their abilities and contributions to the field. Some of these individuals include:

• Bevy Jaegers: An accomplished psychometrist and author, Jaegers established the US Psi Squad, an organisation dedicated to assisting law enforcement agencies with psychic investigations, which included psychometry as one of its primary techniques.

• Stephan A. Schwartz: A parapsychologist and author, Schwartz has conducted numerous experiments and investigations involving psychometry, including the Alexandria Project, which explored the potential use of psychometry in archaeological research.

Objects Commonly Used in Psychometry

A wide variety of objects can be used in psychometry, as long as they have a connection to a person or event. Some commonly used objects include:

• Personal items: Jewellery, watches, clothing, and other personal belongings often carry the energy of their owner, making them ideal for psychometry.

• Antiques and artefacts: Items with historical significance or that have been passed down through generations can provide insight into their history and previous owners.

• Tools and instruments: Objects used regularly by individuals, such as pens, glasses, or musical instruments, can carry the energy of their users.

• Photographs: Images of people or events can also be used in psychometry, as they may hold residual energy related to the subject.

Developing Psychometry Exercise

- Gently cradle an item in the embrace of your palms, feeling every curve and contour of its well-worn surface. This treasure should be one that has been cherished and used by its previous owners, imbued with memories and stories waiting to be unlocked.
- With eyes closed and a few steady relaxing breathes, delve into the mysteries of this object by asking yourself a series of introspective questions.
- What are my first impressions physically, mentally, emotionally and spiritually?
- Who were the hands that held this before you?
- What kind of person were they?
- Are they still alive, or have they journeyed beyond this world?
- As you ponder these queries, allow your senses to guide you through a journey of discovery.
- Perhaps you'll be struck by a wave of emotion or a sudden image, offering glimpses into the life of the owner.

- Listen closely for messages and whispers that may reveal themselves to you.
- If you find yourself struggling to connect, don't give up. Simply return to your questions, asking and exploring until the secrets begin to flow freely.
- Try the exercise on different days and at different times.

In conclusion, psychometry is a fascinating and potentially valuable psychic skill that offers unique insights into the history and energy of objects and their owners. By understanding its benefits, history, and applications, one can appreciate the potential of psychometry as a powerful tool for intuitive readers and investigators alike.

24

DOWSING

Dowsing is an ancient practice that involves the use of tools such as Y-shaped sticks, metal rods, or pendulums to locate objects or substances that are hidden from view.

Dowsing can also be used for health purposes. In fact, dowsing may be able to help you find out about health problems before they become serious, identify food or environmental allergies, and locate energy blockages in the body. Dowsing can also be used to diagnose illnesses and to find the best treatment for them.

The use of dowsing tools is said to be based on the theory that energy fields emanating from objects or other matter, can be precisely located by humans. The dowsing tool acts as a conductor or amplifier. The tool as a conductor is often metal, but crystals and wood are frequently used too. Dowsers are able to add their intuition to a general direction of the energy source, and with their dowsing tools, locate them precisely.

Each method of dowsing has its own unique set of instructions and techniques. Some people believe that dowsing is an innate ability that everyone has, while others believe that it can be learned with practice. Intuitives, don't actually need dowsing tools to locate matter or objects. However, the additional amplification of energy and the intention, all add to success.

Dowsing With A Pendulum

If you're interested in energy, intuition, and expanding your awareness, then read on as we dive into its uses, accuracy, and the technique of pendulum dowsing.

Dowsing has been used for centuries and for various purposes, such as locating water, minerals, or even lost objects. The use of pendulums in dowsing has gained popularity in recent years, primarily due to their simplicity and convenience. With just a small weight suspended from a string or chain, you can tap into your intuition and potentially access hidden knowledge.

Choosing and Using a Pendulum

Pendulums can be made from various materials, such as metal, wood, or crystal, each with its own unique energy and characteristics. To get started with pendulum dowsing, you'll need to choose a pendulum that resonates with you and feels comfortable in your hand.

To dowse with a pendulum, simply hold the chain or string between your thumb and index finger, allowing the weight to hang freely. Find a comfortable, relaxed position, and try to quiet your mind. Focus on the question or subject you're seeking answers to, and begin by asking the pendulum to show you a "yes" or "no" response.

Typically, a pendulum will move in a specific direction or pattern for "yes" or "no" responses, such as clockwise or counter clockwise circles or back and forth swings. These responses can vary between individuals, so it's essential to establish your pendulum's unique language.

Improving Accuracy and Understanding Limitations

Now that you've established a communication with your pendulum, you can begin asking questions or seeking information. Remember that the accuracy of pendulum dowsing relies heavily on the dowser's ability to remain unbiased and open to the answers they receive. It's essential to practice and refine your skills over time.

It's important to note that pendulum dowsing is not a scientifically proven method, and its accuracy is subjective. Many dowsers claim impressive success rates, while sceptics attribute positive outcomes to chance or the ideomotor effect, where subconscious muscle movements influence the pendulum's motion.

Personal Experiences and Taking the First Step

In conclusion, pendulum dowsing is a fascinating practice with a long history and various applications. Whether you're a believer or a sceptic, dowsing can be an enjoyable and intriguing way to explore your intuition and the world around you.

25

TAROT AND ORACLE CARDS AS AN INTUITIVE TOOL

Tarot And Oracle Cards As An Intuitive Tool

Another way to hone our intuition is through the use of tarot or oracle cards. These spiritual tools have been used for centuries to provide guidance, insight, and self-reflection. They can help you develop your intuition and unlock your inner wisdom.

Understanding Tarot and Oracle Cards

Tarot and oracle cards are two distinct systems of divination that serve as tools for insight, self-reflection and personal growth. Tarot comprises 78 cards divided into two groups: the Major Arcana, which represents significant life events, and the Minor Arcana, which deals with everyday matters and may also develop further details around a major card.

Oracle cards are more flexible and can vary in number and theme. Both systems use symbols, images, and archetypes to evoke intuitive insights and empower individuals to make choices that align with their inner truth.

The best way to learn how to work with the cards is to find a teacher, a course or read the many books on the subject. There is much to learn about their history and motivation. Your intuition will develop as you grow with your experience and knowledge of how they can be incorporated into your intuitive practices. However, here are some key aspects to working with intuition and cards:

Build a relationship with the cards

To effectively develop your intuition using tarot and oracle cards, you must first establish a connection with them. Get to know the cards by considering their imagery, meanings, and symbolism. This deepens your understanding of the cards and creates a foundation for interpreting their messages intuitively.

Trusting your instincts

When working with tarot and oracle cards, it's crucial to trust your instincts. Allow your intuition to guide you as you select cards, interpret their meanings, and apply the insights to your life. Over time, you'll develop a stronger sense of trust in your intuitive abilities.

Practicing regularly

Just like any skill, developing intuition through tarot and oracle cards requires practice. Set aside time each day or week to work with your cards, and you'll notice your intuitive abilities growing stronger. Consistent practice helps you become more attuned to the subtle messages and symbols the cards hold.

Reflecting on your readings

After completing a tarot or oracle card reading, take time to reflect on the insights you've gained. Consider how the messages relate to life and what actions you can take to align with your intuition. Journaling about your readings can be an effective way to deepen your understanding and track your progress.

Learning from others

Joining a community of tarot and oracle card enthusiasts can help you develop your intuition and learn from others' experiences. Take part in online forums, attend workshops, or join local meetings to exchange ideas, insights, and techniques.

Tarot and oracle cards are powerful tools that can help you develop your intuition and access your inner wisdom. By building a relationship with the cards, trusting your instincts, practicing regularly, reflecting on your readings, and learning from others, you can unlock the full potential of your intuitive abilities. Embrace the journey of self-discovery and personal growth that tarot and oracle cards can offer, and you'll find yourself empowered to make more authentic, intuitive decisions in every aspect of your life.

26

HOW THE 'CLAIRS' ARE PART OF YOUR INTUITION

Intuition is a natural aspect of human consciousness, allowing us to perceive the world beyond our five physical senses. It enables us to navigate the complexities of life, drawing upon a deep well of internal and external knowledge. One crucial way intuition manifests is through the "Clairs," a series of psychic abilities that enhance our capacity for understanding the world around us. In this chapter, we will explore how the Clairs are intertwined with intuition and how they can deepen our connection with ourselves and others.

Clairvoyance, or clear seeing, is an intuitive ability that enables a person to perceive mental images, symbols, or scenes. These visuals often hold profound significance and can reveal insights or messages from the spirit realm. This ability is a powerful aspect of intuition as it enables a person to access and interpret subtle energies beyond the scope of ordinary perception.

Similarly, clairaudience, or clear hearing, allows a person to receive auditory messages from spirits or other unseen sources. These sounds often carry profound meaning, guiding individuals to make sense of their experiences and emotions. This intuitive ability provides a direct line of communication with the unseen world, enriching our understanding of the spiritual dimensions of existence.

Clairsentience, or clear feeling, is the intuitive capacity to sense emotions, sensations, or impressions related to spirits or situations. This ability connects deeply with the empathic nature of human beings, allowing us to tap into the emotional states of others and develop a more profound understanding of their experiences. By engaging with our clairsentient abilities, we can cultivate greater empathy and emotional intelligence.

Claircognisance, or clear knowing, is an aspect of intuition that grants individuals an innate, unexplainable knowledge about a spirit or situation. This ability bypasses the need for direct communication or sensory perception, providing an immediate and deep understanding of the matter at hand. Claircognisance allows us to access a higher level of wisdom, enabling us to make informed decisions and navigate complex situations with ease.

Clairolfactrience, or clear smelling, is a lesser-known but equally valuable intuitive ability. It allows individuals to perceive scents that trigger memories, emotions, or connections to the spirit world. By recognising and interpreting these olfactory sensations, we can receive messages and guidance from beyond the physical plane.

Finally, clairgustance, or clear tasting, is an intuitive ability that allows a person to detect specific tastes connected to a spirit or situation. This perception can provide valuable insights and enhance our overall understanding of the world around us.

The Clairs are also part of human intuition, allowing us to access and interpret information beyond the limitations of our physical senses. By developing and nurturing these abilities, we can deepen our connection with the eternal consciousness, strengthen our relationships with others, listen to the whisper of the soul - our intuition. Embracing the Clairs is another powerful way to tap into our innate intuitive abilities.

27

MANIFESTING YOUR INTUITION THROUGH THE CLAIRS: EXERCISE

- Find a place to sit where you won't be disturbed for a few minutes.
- Take some calming breaths.
- Focus on your calming breaths and relax your body.
- Create an image in your mind of a perfectly ripe, lemon.
- Just one.
- And I invite you to inspect it.
- Turn it around.
- See all the little pits within the skin.
- Notice its shape.
- And imagine how it feels in your hand.
- The texture.
- The weight.

- And I invite you now to imagine that you are cutting the lemon in half.
- Hear the sound of the knife slicing through to the chopping board.
- You pick up one of the halves of lemon and study it.
- See all the little segments in great detail.
- You see the juice glistening?
- And as you look at the half of lemon.
- Look at it straight on and see all the pips.
- And all the segments within the segments.
- Bring the halved lemon up to your nose and smell it.
- Now, I invite you to imagine that you are holding that half a lemon.
- Up to your mouth and squeezing the juice into your mouth.
- Be aware of taste of the sharpness.
- Be aware of how you react.
- Be aware of how it makes you feel.
- And be aware also in general emotionally.
- How you are feeling at this moment?
- Now, let the image drift away and gently bring your awareness back to yourself to your body and to your environment.

You can repeat this exercise with your eyes closed too

From this simple exercise with imagining a lemon, totally imagining it, you were able to create an image in your mind, an accurate image in your mind and you were able to explore it in detail.

You were also able to explore the texture of it, the weight of it, how it felt, its scent and you were also able to see that image change when you imagine cutting it into.

Physically and emotionally you reacted to that image.

For most of us, what also happens is that when you imagine squeezing lemon juice into your mouth, it begins to fill with saliva.

What's happening is your mind (imagination/thought/suggestion) has created something that has actually made your body physiologically react. Areas of your brain associated with these senses were activated and sent messages to your body - which responded.

That's how powerful you are. Our thoughts are real things!

If you don't get it at first, all of this requires practice and practice and more practice. It does get easier. You do have to put the work in, but it's incredible, isn't it?

Something imagined in your mind, affects your body and you can physiologically react or change.

PART 4: THE INTUITIVE SUPERSTATE

28

BEING SUPERCONSCIOUS

Space between thoughts

Superconscious - the soul gateway

The Superconscious mind is the perceiver of universal truths and universal laws, which will always help an individual no matter what state they are in. It can also be described as a gateway between the intuitive soul and spirit.

The term superconscious (also referred to as the collective unconscious, or higher consciousness) is used to describe that area of the mind where the contents of the entire mind are contained. It is considered by some to be where we always exist spiritually and where we are found after human physical death.

At the deepest intuitive level, the threshold between the soul and the spirit is met here. Exchanges of human experience and spiritual experience evaluate and respond to each other. If the soul experience enlivens the eternal spirit, we are closer to a completeness with the divine, creative life force.

The Superconscious Mind And Intuition: Perceiver of Universal Truths and Laws

The concept of the superconscious mind has been a topic of discussion and exploration for centuries, with roots in various spiritual, philosophical, and psychological disciplines. It is believed to be a higher form of consciousness that allows individuals to access and perceive universal truths and laws.

The superconscious mind is often considered a bridge between the individual's soul and the greater spiritual realm. It is through the superconscious that one can tap into a higher plane of existence, gaining insights into the universal principles that govern our lives. In doing so, the individual becomes more connected to their spiritual self and attains a heightened sense of awareness and understanding.

Theories and Perspectives on the Superconscious Mind

Swiss psychiatrist Carl Jung proposed the idea of the collective unconscious, a shared reservoir of universal knowledge, symbols, and archetypes that transcends personal experience. While distinct from the superconscious mind, the collective unconscious can be seen as a parallel concept, suggesting a level of consciousness that provides access to higher knowledge and wisdom.

Spiritual and Mystical Traditions

In various spiritual and mystical traditions, the superconscious mind is also referred to as the "Higher Self" or the "Universal Mind." These traditions propose that the superconscious mind can provide access to divine knowledge and wisdom, guiding individuals on their spiritual journeys.

Integral Theory

Ken Wilber's Integral Theory, a comprehensive framework for understanding human consciousness and development, includes the concept of the "subtle" and "causal" levels of consciousness. These levels are believed to correspond to the superconscious mind, allowing individuals to access and embody universal truths and laws.

While empirical research on the superconscious mind is limited, studies in related areas such as altered states of consciousness, transpersonal psychology, and meditation suggest potential avenues for understanding the superconscious mind's nature and functioning.

Research on altered states of consciousness, such as those achieved through meditation or psychedelics, has provided some insights into the potential workings of the superconscious mind. These altered states are often characterised by a sense of unity with the universe and access to deeper levels of understanding and wisdom.

Transpersonal Psychology

Transpersonal psychology, a branch of psychology focused on transcendent and spiritual experiences, offers another perspective on the superconscious mind. Through the study of mystical and peak experiences, transpersonal psychology seeks to understand the higher realms of human consciousness, which may include the superconscious mind.

Meditation and Mindfulness And The Superconscious

Meditation and mindfulness practices have long been associated with accessing higher states of consciousness. Research in these areas has shown that regular practice can lead to enhanced self-awareness, emotional regulation, and a greater sense of interconnectedness with others and the world at large, which may indicate the superconscious mind's influence.

The superconscious mind, as the perceiver of universal truths and laws, offers individuals a unique opportunity to connect with the greater spiritual realm and access deep, transformative wisdom. As we continue to explore the superconscious mind, we may unlock a greater understanding of ourselves, our place in the universe, and the profound wisdom that lies beyond our ordinary experiences.

Understanding and accessing the superconscious mind can have a profound impact on an individual's personal growth, self-awareness, and spiritual development. Some practical applications of the superconscious mind include:

- Enhanced Creativity

By tapping into the superconscious mind, individuals can access a wellspring of creativity and inspiration. This heightened state of consciousness can enable artists, writers, and other creative professionals to produce innovative and original work.

- Problem Solving and Decision Making

Accessing the superconscious mind can provide insights and solutions to complex problems that may seem insurmountable from a conventional perspective. Through intuitive understanding of universal laws, individuals can make better-informed decisions that align with their values and goals.

- Personal Growth and Transformation

Connecting with the superconscious mind can facilitate personal growth and transformation, as individuals gain access to higher wisdom and understanding. This heightened state of consciousness can lead to the development of greater empathy, compassion, and a sense of interconnectedness with others and the world at large.

- Spiritual Development

As the superconscious mind serves as a bridge between the individual's soul and the greater spiritual realm, tapping into this higher consciousness can deepen one's spiritual journey. Through regular practice and self-reflection, individuals can develop a greater sense of inner peace, purpose, and connection to the divine.

Common Techniques for Accessing the Superconscious Mind

While the superconscious mind may seem elusive, various techniques and practices are thought to facilitate access to this higher state of consciousness. Some of these methods include:

- Meditation

Meditation is a time-tested practice that can quiet the conscious mind and allow individuals to access the superconscious mind. Techniques such as mindfulness, transcendental meditation, and loving-kindness meditation can help individuals develop greater self-awareness and connect with their inner wisdom.

- Contemplative Prayer

Contemplative prayer, practiced in various spiritual traditions, is another method of accessing the superconscious mind. Through focused intention and deep connection with the divine, individuals can experience a heightened state of awareness and spiritual insight.

- Visualisation and Guided Imagery

Visualisation and guided imagery can help individuals tap into the superconscious mind by creating mental images that evoke feelings of peace, tranquility, and connection to the universe. These practices can facilitate access to deeper levels of understanding and wisdom.

- Mindfulness and Present Moment Awareness

Cultivating mindfulness and present moment awareness can help individuals access the superconscious mind by quieting the chatter of the conscious mind and fostering a deeper connection with the self and the world around them.

The Superconscious Mind and Intuition

The superconscious mind is closely related to our intuition, as both involve accessing insights and knowledge that lie beyond our ordinary conscious awareness. Intuition can be understood as the innate ability to grasp information, decide, or form judgments without relying solely on logic or conscious reasoning. It is often described as a "gut feeling" or an "inner knowing." The relationship between the superconscious mind and intuition can be explored through the following aspects:

The superconscious mind, as the perceiver of universal truths and laws, can be considered the source of intuitive insights. By tapping into the superconscious mind, individuals can access a reservoir of deep wisdom and understanding that informs their intuitive abilities. This connection allows them to decide and judgments that are aligned with their inner values and higher purpose.

Both the superconscious mind and intuition involve a heightened state of awareness. Accessing the superconscious mind can enhance an individual's intuition by opening them up to higher levels of consciousness and understanding. This expanded awareness allows individuals to perceive subtle cues, patterns, and connections that might otherwise be missed by the conscious mind.

Developing a strong connection with the superconscious mind can help individuals trust their intuition. As they become more attuned to the insights and wisdom offered by the superconscious mind, they can learn to rely on their intuitive abilities as a valuable source of guidance and direction in their lives.

Many of the practices and techniques that facilitate access to the superconscious mind, such as meditation, mindfulness, and visualisation, can also enhance and develop intuition. By regularly engaging in these practices, individuals can strengthen the connection between the superconscious mind and their intuitive abilities, leading to more accurate and insightful decision-making.

The superconscious mind is intimately connected to our intuition, providing a source of deep wisdom and understanding that informs our intuitive abilities. By accessing the superconscious mind, individuals can develop a heightened state of awareness that allows them to trust and rely on their intuition as a powerful tool for decision-making, problem-solving, and personal growth.

29

ACADEMIC ACCEPTANCE OF INTUITION

The fact that academics have researched intuition, suggests that there is consensus that it is a force to be reckoned with. Intuition captures the attention of curious minds and is researched mostly, by psychologists and anthropologists. Academic insights include:

Intuition can be thought of as insight that arises spontaneously without conscious reasoning. Daniel Kahneman, who won a Nobel prize in economics for his work on human judgment and decision-making, has proposed that we have two different thought systems: system 1 is fast and intuitive; system 2 is slower and relies on reasoning. The fast system, he holds, is more prone to error. It has its place: it may increase the chance of survival by enabling us to anticipate serious threats and recognize promising opportunities. But the slower thought system, by engaging critical thinking and analysis, is less susceptible to producing bad decisions. [1]

Also:

It was discovered that managers at a food company use intuition in their work. Almost all of them stated that, in addition to rational analyses, they tapped gut feelings when making decisions. More than half tended to lean on rational approaches; about a quarter used a strategy that blended rational and intuitive elements; and about a fifth generally relied on intuition alone. Interestingly, the more upper-level managers tended more toward intuition, although those closer to the bottom of the ladder leaned more toward a balanced blend between rational analysis and gut feelings! [2]

Russel Fulcher explains in his blog about intuition that:

Gut feelings or intuitions come from patterns we've identified in our past experiences. Your subconscious mind continuously processes information that you are not consciously aware of, not only when you're asleep but also when you're awake. This helps explain the "aha" moments you experience when you see, feel, hear or learn something that you actually already knew. The revelation of the obvious occurs **when your conscious mind finally learns something that your subconscious mind had already known.**[3]

We can be in no doubt that intuition has inspired many great academic minds. Gerd Gigerenzer - The Author of 'Gut Feelings: The Intelligence of the Unconscious'

"In my scientific work, I have hunches. I can't explain always why I think a certain path is the right way, but I need to trust it and go ahead. I also have the ability to check these hunches and find out what they are about. That's the science part. Now, in private life, I rely on instinct. For instance, when I first met my wife, I didn't do computations. Nor did she."[4]

~

1. **Thinking Fast and Slow.** Daniel Kahneman. Farrar, Straus and Giroux, 2011
2. **Intuition in Decision Making--Theoretical and Empirical Aspects.** Kamila Malewska in *Business and Management Review,* Vol. 6, No. 3, pages 23–31; June 2015.
3. https://www.russellfutcher.com/new-blog/2022/2/14/the-psychology-of-intuition-trusting-your-gut#:
4. https://www.goodreads.com/book/show/786560.Gut_Feelings

PART 5: 11 TIPS FOR DEVELOPING YOUR INTUITIVE READING ABILITY

Getting in Touch with Your Soul and Clearing the Mind

I. The first step in giving intuitive readings is to connect with your inner self and clear your mind. This will help you become a more open and receptive channel for intuitive information.

1. Meditation: Practice regular meditation to calm your thoughts, increase self-awareness, and enhance your intuition.

2. Breathing exercises: Engage in deep, mindful breathing to release tension and improve mental clarity.

3. Grounding: Connect with the earth and your physical body to anchor your energy and remain present during readings.

II. Awareness of Gut Feelings

Pay attention to your gut feelings or instincts, as they often provide accurate intuitive guidance.

1. Practice mindfulness: Cultivate an awareness of your feelings, thoughts, and bodily sensations.

2. Trust your instincts: Believe in your intuitive abilities and don't second-guess your gut feelings.

3. Develop discernment: Learn to distinguish between intuition and fear or wishful thinking.

III. The Clairs: Clairvoyance, Clairsentience, Clairaudience, and Claircognisance

Develop your psychic senses to enhance your intuitive abilities.

1. Clairvoyance (clear seeing): Practice visualisation exercises to strengthen your ability to receive mental images.

2. Clairsentience (clear feeling): Pay attention to physical sensations and emotions that provide intuitive information.

3. Clairaudience (clear hearing): Listen carefully to sounds and voices that may hold intuitive messages.

4. Claircognisance (clear knowing): Trust sudden insights or ideas that seem to come from nowhere.

IV. Physical, Emotional, Mental, and Spiritual Aspects

Consider all aspects of a person's energy state, or for a situation or for yourself, when giving intuitive readings.

1. Physical: Assess the physical body intuitively, including imbalances and energy levels.

2. Emotional: Explore emotions and feelings, both current, past and going forward.

3. Mental: Examine thought patterns, beliefs, and attitudes.

4. Spiritual: Delve into the individual's spiritual journey, life purpose, and soul lessons.

V. The Chakra System

Use knowledge of the chakra system to gain insight into a person's energy flow and overall well-being.

1. Learn the chakra locations and functions: Familiarise yourself with the seven main chakras and their corresponding aspects.

2. Detect imbalances: Use intuition, pendulum, or other methods to identify blocked or overactive chakras.

3. Suggest healing techniques: Offer recommendations for balancing and healing the chakras, such as meditation, crystals, or energy work. However, recommend that for any health concerns they must consult a qualified doctor.

VI. Tarot and Oracle Cards

Incorporate tarot and oracle cards as tools for accessing intuitive guidance.

1. Learn the basics: Study the meanings and symbolism of the cards.

2. Develop your intuition: Trust your intuition when interpreting the cards and allow for personal insights.

3. Create a sacred space: Set up a quiet, comfortable area for conducting readings.

VII. Body Scan Technique

Use the body scan technique to identify areas of tension, discomfort, or imbalance within the body.

1. Guided meditation: Lead yourself through a meditation that focuses on each part of the body in turn.

2. Intuitive insights: Note any intuitive information that arises during the body scan.

3. Suggestions for healing: Offer recommendations for addressing any issues detected during the scan.

VIII. Dowsing

Employ dowsing techniques, such as using a pendulum, to receive intuitive guidance, or detect changes in energy fields.

1. Choose a tool: Select a pendulum or another dowsing instrument that resonates with you.

2. Develop your skill: Practice asking clear, concise questions and interpreting the responses accurately.

3. Incorporate intuition: Use your intuitive abilities to enhance the dowsing process and provide deeper insights.

IX. Reading the Aura

Learn to perceive and interpret the human energy field or aura.

1. Develop auric vision: Train your eyes to see the subtle energy field around people by practicing exercises such as gazing and un-focusing your eyes.

2. Understand colours and patterns: Familiarise yourself with the meanings of different aura colours and patterns, which can provide insight into a person's emotional, mental, and spiritual state.

3. Combine intuition: Use your intuitive abilities to further interpret the information gathered from reading the aura.

X. Regularly practice self-compassion.

Self-compassion is the practice of treating oneself with kindness, understanding, and empathy, especially during times of suffering or personal setbacks. It is a crucial element of emotional well-being, as it helps individuals cope with difficult emotions and promotes self-care. Here are some steps to help you practice self-compassion effectively:

1. Acknowledge your feelings: The first step in practicing self-compassion is to recognize and accept your emotions, without judgment. It's important to allow yourself to feel your emotions, as denying them can lead to further emotional distress. Be honest with yourself about what you're feeling and why.

2. Treat yourself as you would treat a friend: We often extend empathy and support to friends during difficult times but struggle to offer the same kindness to ourselves. When you're going through a challenging situation, imagine what you would say or do to help a friend in the same situation, and then apply that same care and understanding to yourself.

3. Practice mindfulness: Mindfulness involves paying attention to the present moment in a non-judgmental way. By being mindful of your thoughts and emotions, you can better understand your feelings and respond

to them with self-compassion. You can practice mindfulness through meditation, deep breathing exercises, or simply taking a moment to observe your thoughts without judgment.

4. Develop self-compassion affirmations: Create and repeat positive affirmations to remind yourself to be compassionate and understanding toward yourself. Some examples include, "I am worthy of love and compassion," "It's okay to make mistakes," and "I forgive myself for my imperfections."

5. Learn from your mistakes: Self-compassion involves recognising that everyone makes mistakes and that setbacks are a natural part of the learning process. Instead of dwelling on your mistakes, use them as opportunities for growth and self-improvement.

6. Set realistic expectations: Unrealistic expectations can lead to feelings of inadequacy and self-criticism. It's important to set achievable goals and recognize that nobody is perfect. Be kind to yourself by acknowledging your limitations and appreciating your progress.

7. Take care of your physical well-being: Self-compassion also involves attending to your physical needs. Get enough sleep, eat well, and engage in regular exercise to support your overall well-being.

8. Surround yourself with compassionate people: The people you surround yourself with can have a significant impact on your ability to practice self-compassion. Seek friends and loved ones who are empathetic, supportive, and understanding, as their compassion can help reinforce your own self-compassionate behaviours.

Remember, self-compassion is a skill that takes practice and patience. By incorporating these tips into your daily life, you can cultivate a kinder, more empathetic relationship with yourself, which will ultimately lead to improved emotional awareness, intuitive receptiveness, well-being and resilience.

XI. Psychometry

Practice psychometry often. Hold an object that has some history or even a crystal. Clear you mind and focus on the breath for a minute or two. Then allow your intuitive senses to get to work. Keep an awareness of emotions, the 'clairs,' the physical, mental and any spiritual aspect. Allow anything that arises in your mind, body and soul relating to the object to manifest.

By developing and refining these skills and techniques, you can become a more effective and compassionate intuitive reader. Remember that practice and self-awareness are key to enhancing your abilities, and always approach your readings with an open heart and a desire to be of service to yourself and others.

30

LEARNING TO STRUCTURE AN
INTUITIVE READING

Every intuitive reader will develop their unique style and skills over time and practice. The following is a starting point, or an opportunity to review your own methods and add any useful aspects to your intuitive work.

An ideal way to structure an intuitive reading for someone else involves creating a comfortable and supportive environment, setting clear intentions, and following an approach that allows for the exploration of various aspects of the sitter's life. Over time, your own intuition will guide the reading.

Here is a suggested structure for an intuitive reading:

Preparation:

- Create a calm and inviting atmosphere for the reading. Ensure the space is clean, quiet, and comfortable.
- Ground yourself and clear your energy. Engage in meditation or visualisation exercises to centre yourself and connect with your intuition.
- Set a clear intention for the reading, focusing on providing guidance, support, and insight for the person you are reading for.

- Establish rapport:
- Welcome the sitter warmly and make them feel at ease.
- Explain the process of the reading and your approach as an intuitive reader.
- Encourage the sitter to be open and receptive, reminding them that the reading is a collaborative process.
- Gathering intention:
- Ask the sitter if they have a specific area of their life they would like to focus on or any particular questions they want to explore.
- Use your preferred method(s) of accessing intuitive information, such as clairvoyance, clairsentience, tarot cards, or psychometry, to gather insights related to the person's situation.
- Be open to any additional information that comes through during the reading, as it may be relevant to the sitter's current circumstances or future path.
- Share your insights:
- Present the information you have gathered in a clear, organised, and compassionate manner.

- Validate the sitter's feelings and experiences, offering support and encouragement as needed.
- Be mindful of how the information is delivered, ensuring it is respectful and empowering for them.
- Offer practical suggestions or action steps in the context of intuitive information, which the sitter can take away, to address their concerns, or move forward in their life.
- Encourage the sitter to trust their intuition and inner wisdom when making decisions or considering the guidance provided.
- Remind the sitter that they have the power to create positive change in their life and that the reading is just one tool to help them along their journey.
- Closing the reading:
- Ask the sitter if they have any final questions or need clarification on any aspect of the reading.
- Thank them for allowing you to read for them and express your appreciation for the opportunity to be of service.
- Close the reading by releasing any energies or connections made during the session, and invite the sitter to take a moment to ground

themselves before leaving the space. A glass of water nearby is ideal to offer them.

By following a considered approach, you can create a meaningful and empowering intuitive reading that provides valuable insights and guidance for the sitter you are reading for. Remember, practice and self-awareness are essential for refining your skills and becoming a more effective intuitive reader.

AFTERWORD: EMBRACING THE POWER OF INTUITION AND ITS LIMITLESS POTENTIAL

As we come to the end of this journey through "The Anatomy of Intuition - Nurturing Your Soul's Gift" it is my hope that you have gained a deeper understanding of the many facets of intuition and discovered practical ways to cultivate this innate gift. Like any skill, developing intuition requires dedication, practice, and patience. As you nurture your intuitive abilities, you will find that they become an invaluable source of guidance, inspiration, and wisdom in your life.

The human experience is rich and multifaceted, and our intuition serves as a bridge connecting us to the unseen realms of consciousness, energy, and spirit. By recognising the importance of intuition and embracing its potential, we can tap into a wellspring of inner wisdom that can guide us through life's challenges and uncertainties.

As you continue on your path of intuitive growth, remember to approach each step with an open heart, a curious mind, and a willingness to explore the boundless landscape of your inner being. Trust in the process, and know that you are not alone on this journey. Countless others have walked the path of intuitive awakening before you, and many more will follow in your footsteps.

Do not be discouraged if your progress seems too slow or if you encounter obstacles along the way. These challenges are an essential part of the learning process and often serve as catalysts for profound growth and transformation. Embrace the lessons they bring, and allow yourself to be guided by the wisdom of your intuition.

As you nurture your intuitive abilities, you may find that your relationships, career, and personal well-being are all positively impacted. Intuition has the power to enrich every aspect of our lives, from the mundane to the extraordinary. By developing your innate soul gift, you can create a life that is more authentic, fulfilling, and deeply connected to the world around you.

In closing, I encourage you to continue exploring the vast landscape of intuition and to share your insights and experiences with others. By doing so, you will not only enrich your own life but also contribute to the collective awakening of humanity's intuitive potential.

May your journey be filled with wonder, growth, and an ever-deepening connection to the wisdom of your intuitive heart.

GLOSSARY

- Alchemy: Any seemingly magical act involving the combining of elements into something new
- Apports: Objects that materialise in a seance room from elsewhere
- Arthur Findlay College (AFC): A world renowned Spiritualist college of psychic sciences
- Attunement: Relates to a state of energetic spiritual harmony
- Cartomancy: Divination with playing cards
- Clairvoyance: Images in the mind
- Clairaudience: Sounds, words or phrases in the mind
- Clairsentience: Sensing information

- Claircognisance: Sensing knowledge
- Clairolfactrience: Sensing an aroma
- Clairgustance: Sensing a taste
- Cognitive: Reasoning, knowing
- Discarnate: Without a body
- Divination: The art of practice, that seeks hidden knowledge, through extra sensory perception. Often involves tools such as reading the tarot, or pendulums.
- Ectoplasm: A substance exuded by the medium to create forms within physical mediumship
- ESi - Emotional, Social, intelligence
- Evidential medium: Someone who communicates with the deceased and provides evidence of their continued existence
- Hermeticism: Hermeticism is a philosophical system that is largely based on the purported teachings of Hermes Trismegistus, the legendary fusion of the Greek god Hermes and Egyptian god Thoth.
- Incarnate: With a physical body
- Mental mediumship: Mind to mind communication and subject to the influence of the mind of both parties. This is the most common form of mediumship

- Mental Synthesis: The process of combining stored visual information to create new images that have not been previously seen or experienced.
- Objective clairvoyance: Experiencing as if the vision is physically present
- Physical mediumship: the phenomenon of spirit is objective and physical. It will be observed by all and not subject to the mind of either sitter of medium
- Precognition: Having foreknowledge, through extra sensory perception, before it happens.
- Prophesy: Interchangeable with precognition but tends to be related to predicting major events.
- Psychic medium: The psychic medium is someone who interprets the energy of a living being or earthly object and communicates the impressions received through their senses.
- Psychic Readings: an intuitive reading of the energy relating to situations or personality traits etc.
- Psychometry: Intuitively, reading the residual energy of objects.

- Rappings: Tapping or knocking sounds purportedly made from a spirit, as a means of communication
- Seance: A seance is a gathering (usually with a medium present) for the purposes of spirit communication
- Second Sight: Another term for clairvoyance
- Sitter: A person/client receiving a 'sitting' with an intuitive/psychic/evidential medium or present in a seance/circle
- Sitting: A meeting between a medium and a sitter
- Subjectively clairvoyant: experiencing the vision within the mind
- Spirit guide: a spiritual archetype assigned only to you, to assist your spiritual progress
- Tarot: Divination cards, originated from a renaissance card game, and featuring archetypes and life events, for interpretation by a tarot reader.

BIBLIOGRAPHY AND RESOURCES

Bringhurst, Robert. *The Elements of Typographic Style*. Version 3.2.
Point Roberts: Hartley & Marks, 2004.

The Chicago Manual of Style. 17th ed. The University of Chicago
Press Editorial Staff. Chicago: The University of Chicago Press,
2017. https://www.chicagomanualofstyle.org/.

https://www.heartmath.org/

https://www.goodreads.com/book/show/786560.Gut_Feelings

Downloads: https://developingspirit.com/course-detail/chakra-
power-exercise/1448

ABOUT THE AUTHOR

Helen DaVita is a Writer, Teacher & Mentor of spiritual development and mediumship. This is Helen's fifth book.

Helen is an experienced writer, teacher, and course creator, who has been recognised globally for her work in personal and spiritual development. With a teaching style that emphasises the importance of honouring one's best self, Helen has inspired students in venues across the UK, Europe, Africa, Asia, USA, and Australia. In addition to her work as a teacher and course organiser at Arthur Findlay College, Helen has also developed enriching learning programmes for students of all levels. She is an approved training provider for the IICT. Her 'sitting in the power' course is globally regarded amongst the finest spiritual development exercises.

For online courses, blogs, audio, videos and ebooks, please take a look at https://developingspirit.com

Printed in Great Britain
by Amazon

40123168R00155